The Warrior Mama

—•— ⛤ —•—

Tidbits and Tales from the Trails

The cover photo was taken in Glacier National Park. Karen's parents, Bev and Stan Fisher, taught her to be a warrior in whatever challenges she faced in life. They have always been her protectors and guides! This first outing was affirmation that life would go on and to keep looking forward. God is already there!

The Warrior Mama

Tidbits and Tales from the Trails

Karen Fisher Ball

Copyright © 2021 Karen Fisher Ball

Cover photo by Kirk Ball
Back cover photo by Rick Guidotti, Positive Exposure

All rights reserved. No part of this book may be reproduced, distributed, or transmitted in any form or by any means, or stored in a database or retrieval system, without the prior written permission of the publisher.

Additional copies of *The Warrior Mama* may be ordered at sturge-weber.org.

Published by The Sturge-Weber Foundation
Houston, Texas

ISBN 978-0-9670484-2-0 (print)
ISBN 978-0-9670484-3-7 (eBook)

Printed in the United States of America

Dedication

I'm eternally grateful to ALL my family members who have supported me in every way and for their own unique additions to make this faith-filled journey bearable and memorable. Each of you knows the part you played and how much I cherish you.

This book is first and foremost dedicated to Kaelin and to those individuals, families, and the research community impacted by a birthmark or Sturge-Weber diagnosis. Without you and your courage to fight another day and share your wisdom, the GNAQ R13 gene discovery would not have been possible. That discovery by researchers Dr. Jonathan Pevsner, Dr. Doug Marchuk, and Dr. Anne Comi (with skillful investigative talents by Dr. Matt Shirley), and funded by the Sturge-Weber Foundation and the Brain Vascular Malformation Consortium in 2013, would have been almost unthinkable a generation ago. It DOES take courage to face the unknown and the countless public stares from the uneducated masses. You inspire me every day to keep striving towards answers, cures, and a better quality of life for all of us. YOU are the heroes of this war I've been waging with Sturge-Weber syndrome since 1986!

The many dedicated staff and volunteers over the years kept the ship afloat too. The many fellow Warrior Mamas I've met have been such deeply influential guides and cheerleaders. Thank you for sharing your lives, your hearts, your talents, and your souls with me. This book is also dedicated to the men who have waged war right along side them. We all bring a mindset and the armor needed to

SWF's first Medical Advisory Board.

win the war on whichever battlefield is in front of us on any given day! Battle On!

The caring and dedicated health care professionals and researchers who took the time to enlighten me about the pathogenesis, many facets of Sturge-Weber syndrome, and treatment options for removing Port Wine birthmarks have been invaluable to my curiosity and understanding. Dr. Jonathan Pevsner, aka "the Admiral" (who I swear is my angel on this earth!), has taught me more about faith and grace and continually reminds me through his words and deeds to be kind.

The many dedicated staff and officials at the National Institutes of Health's National Center for Advancing Translational Sciences (NCATS)-Office of Rare Disease especially, as well as the Food and Drug Administration's Office of Rare Diseases, Pediatrics, Urologic and Reproductive Medicine (ORPURM), have been wonderfully patient teachers and advisors. Together, we have improved lives and soldiered on when we were weary because we were called to do God's work. You can try and say no to God but He will ALWAYS prevail in all things!

This book is also dedicated to my Daddy, Stan Fisher, MOO, Mighty Omnipotent One. His sense of humor and self-deprecation makes our lives a laugh a minute even in the midst of pathos or sorrow.

Dedication

Knights in Shining Armor: My Band of Brothers—or is it The Three Stooges!

It is because of his loving presence and unending belief in my abilities that the Sturge-Weber Foundation (The SWF) exists. It is also dedicated to my Mama, Bev Fisher. She has been his "straight man" and "stylish maven" for sixty-eight years and nurtures us along the way. Her unending faith, creativity, love of the arts, and master cooking skills—combined with her belief in "there IS a plan"—uplifts us all.

I am also grateful for my brothers who have a special piece of Daddy in each of them. I have a plaque that reads, "Home is where your story begins." True story! Lastly, I'm grateful for my dear friend, Pat S., who knocked on my door and spread sunshine and an invitation I couldn't refuse to join the cherished women at Clearview Community Church. My New Jersey and Colorado girlfriends, how you make me laugh! Your support in speaking about my faith as a personal relationship which honors God and my family is such a blessing. You truly helped me publish this book and "birth it Martha," as ol' MOO says!

The Sturge-Weber Foundation (SWF) is the place where, for children born with Sturge-Weber syndrome and other port wine birthmark conditions and for their loved ones, their personal war stories unfold with shared experiences, tears, and laughter as they build up an arsenal of knowledge and hope. Each personal battle with SWS is unique, but the SWF unites us to win the war! Thanks to your purchase of this book they will have a home to turn to which is filled with knowledge, hope, laughter, and a stronger foundation for today, tomorrow, and until a cure is found. With faith, hope, and love.... Karen

Table of Contents

DEDICATION • V | FOREWORD • XIII
PREFACE • XVII | INTRODUCTION • XXI

PART I: FAMILY

CHAPTER 1: FAITH AND FAMILY • 1
CHAPTER 2: WHISPERS AND IMPRINTS ON MY HEART • 43
CHAPTER 3: HOLY SMOKES! YOU WANT ME TO DO WHAT? • 55

PART II: WARRIOR MAMAS

CHAPTER 4: INSPIRATIONAL WARRIOR MAMA STORIES • 67
SARA'S WARRIOR MAMA • 68
SUMMER'S WARRIOR MAMA • 69
LUKA'S WARRIOR MAMA • 71
WARRIOR MAMA'S NOTE TO YOUNGER SELF • 73
SILAS' WARRIOR MAMA • 74
STEPHEN'S WARRIOR MAMA • 77
CÉLINE'S WARRIOR MAMA • 79
MARISSA'S WARRIOR MAMA • 83
DANNY'S WARRIOR MAMA • 85
MYLA'S WARRIOR MAMA • 90
MILLIE'S WARRIOR MAMA • 93
SWF'S CHERISHED WARRIOR MAMA • 97

PART III: ALLIES
CHAPTER 5: THE NIH AND THE FDA • 103
CHAPTER 6: SCIENCE: BENCH TO BEDSIDE • 109
CHAPTER 7: NOW WHAT! • 113
CHAPTER 8: HOW GREAT THOU ART! • 119

PART IV: TALES FROM THE TRAILS
CHAPTER 9: TIDBITS, TIPS, AND TALES FROM THE TRAILS • 125
LIL' DITTIES TO GET YOU THROUGH THE DAY • 126
MUSINGS AND TALES FROM THE WARRIOR MAMA • 128
THEY SAID! • 129
HEAL YOUR HEART AND HEAL YOUR HEAD! • 130
NOTHING GOOD HAPPENS AFTER 12 MIDNIGHT OR 12 NOON! • 132
CARRY YOUR WATER • 134
THE PATH YOU HAVE BEEN GIVEN • 135
JUST REMEMBER • 136
THE VICTIM OR THE VICTOR? • 139
MY GRAMMA'S CHAIRS ... CELEBRATING LIFE, LOSS, AND THE FAITH THAT SEES US THROUGH IT • 140
ANGELS AMONG US! • 144
LESSONS FROM GEESE • 145
WEEDS ... GOTTA LOVE 'EM! • 148
ROADBLOCKS TO RESCUE • 149
I'M A LANYARD LOVER ... AND I GIVE THANKS! • 151
LOVE IN THE TIME OF CORONA, COVID-19, OR CHINA • 152
FREEDOM ISN'T FREE! • 154
BE WORTHY! • 156
WHIPPING OR WHISPERING WINDS ... THE STORMS OF LIFE! • 158
SEED MONEY AND YOU: THE RIPPLING IMPACT • 160
PART 1: THE RIPPLING IMPACT OF NETWORKING • 161
PART 2: THE RIPPLING IMPACT OF COLLABORATION AND RESEARCH • 164

Table of Contents

PART 3: THE RIPPLING IMPACT OF INVESTING
IN INFRASTRUCTURE • 171
PART 4: THE FUTURE HARVEST • 174
ON THE ROAD OF LIFE AND LOVE • 176
YOUR PERSONAL DAY OF INFAMY OR EPIPHANY • 178
THE ONLY RECIPE TO REMEMBER! • 180

AFTERWORD • 183

ABOUT THE STURGE-WEBER FOUNDATION • 188

Foreword

by Tina S. Alster, MD

When I opened my medical practice thirty years ago armed with a pioneering laser to ease the burden of disfiguring birthmarks for my patients, I was forced to recognize that despite such technology, this promising instrument was not a magic wand. As in other areas of medicine, some conditions stubbornly resisted treatment and many were accompanied by far more serious realities.

It was in this context of medical and scientific advances that I came face-to-face with Sturge-Weber syndrome (SWS). The more I learned about and encountered this condition, the more I realized it would be a long and arduous road in order to significantly ease the burden on affected patients and their families.

It is with this in mind that I am drawn to *The Warrior Mama: Tidbits and Tales from the Trails* by Karen Fisher Ball. This is an immensely readable book that invites us on the journey that Karen and so many others have, through fate, been traveling.

I have known Karen since early in my professional career and have witnessed her roller-coaster ride as she has fought the battles inherent in focusing attention on and promoting awareness of Sturge-Weber syndrome. I and many of my medical colleagues have been involved in a variety of ways and over many years in support of the Sturge-Weber Foundation. We have worked closely with Karen, embraced patients and their families, actively educated others, and championed the advancement of therapeutic research—all in an effort to provide better care and treatments for SWS.

Dr. Alster (center) and our dedicated stellar dermatologists.

Despite my personal and professional interest, I know I cannot have a full appreciation of Sturge-Weber and its broad impact because I am looking through a practitioner's lens. Karen's book narrows this gap considerably. That alone merits a serious read. In addition, we see first-hand the true trials of those affected most—patients, families, and caregivers.

Although Karen's story and that of her daughter, Kaelin, are at the heart of this book, they are no less the means to draw into it a variety of people in common cause, as well as those who need to learn about Sturge-Weber syndrome and the daunting, never-ending challenges it poses. Karen is the beacon of this narrative as she leads us beyond her immediate role and experiences to those who lovingly care for family members with SWS. Her dedication to overcoming the daunting hardship faced by her daughter is, along with other personal stories, truly inspirational.

Chapters on Sturge-Weber, the role of federal government agencies, and the invaluable research they fund serve to encourage us about what has been accomplished to date—and to spur us on to support much more research. Karen's perspectives and insights about endless networking are a reminder of the ceaseless quest to end the individual burden through increased and broader funding at home and abroad.

This is not just a book about Karen nor Kaelin (and others like her). *The Warrior Mama* is a book that is at once inspirational, honest in its presentation, and straightforward in its outline for ongoing and future work. It challenges me as a physician—as well as those in positions of political leadership and in senior government agencies who have it within their power—to do more.

I hope this book will serve as a meaningful introduction to a wider audience of families who are directly affected by Sturge-Weber syndrome and searching for a common bond. I also hope it will serve to bring a far greater awareness of SWS and its deep-seated impact on affected individuals and communities. Lastly, this is a book for policymakers to reference in order to garner support for additional funding and more timely research.

Karen Fisher Ball is not only a Warrior Mama of long standing, but she is also the voice of the good angel on our shoulder bringing us patiently—by thought, word, and deed—to a better place.

Tina S. Alster, MD
Washington Institute of Dermatologic Laser Surgery
June 2021

Preface

I've come full circle. I became a Warrior Mama on October 11, 1986. It seems a lifetime ago but in truth it has been thirty-five years and the time has gone so quickly. My return to Aurora, Colorado in the summer of 2015 was the culmination of a lifetime of joyous celebrations, tearful tirades, and miraculous moments. Little did I know that fateful morning when they placed Kaelin, my first child and daughter, in my arms that the Holy Spirit and a patient God would lead me down a path of unimaginable trials and celebrations of faith, hope, and love. Kaelin has been my sidekick, joy, and inspiration ever since her "birth" day! That's when a lifetime of Daddy's teachings and sense of humor truly saved me from despair and self-pity, and supported me on the frontlines of my personal war with Sturge-Weber syndrome (SWS).

I don't think the transformation in me as a woman, a wife, a mother, and as a woman of faith is that unusual, because we each have a unique gift that God gives us—but it's up to us to nurture and honor that gift.

This is a story that has been long in the telling. I've resisted telling it for a variety of reasons: "It's right to be humble," "It's not a good time now," and myriad other excuses running around in my head in response to the Holy Spirit's persistent whisper on my heart. This book actually came to me as two books ... one about my family and our deep roots in faith and service, and another about the professional highlights and folks I met along the way. As I was closing down our home in New Jersey, preparing the next chapter of life, I realized the two cannot be separated in the telling. As a faithful follower it would be disingenuous to not acknowledge the role God has played in our lives AND this war on Sturge-Weber syndrome. Someone would have come along and stepped up to help other families with SWS challenges. My family's faith and examples of how to live an impactful life through service to others just made it inevitable that we would take action! There are still so many in dire need of help and support with answers through research! I have many more battles to wage and conquer before getting off the frontlines.

I truly understand and respect the position that some may not pick up this book because it is faith-based or are turned off by the war terminology. There are many ways to discuss or even label what faith means or how it is followed. There are also many ways and people needed to fight a war, and without warriors willing to go to the front lines on our behalf, where would we be? Dr. Sturge and Dr. Weber were our first frontline soldiers when they first identified the enemy in the 1870s and early 1900s. The pharmaceutical and device makers developed an arsenal of tools for doctors over the years to care for those on the front lines. Researchers never gave up and we've all been called in some manner to bring answers and joy to those suffering. I am proud to have served with all the patients, my friends, and colleagues. All of us have been blessed to serve and share our witness to that faith.

Why a *Warrior Mama* you may ask? Well, let's just say that too was revealed after a serendipitous encounter that left me speechless. I was at a biotech conference and listening to a lecture from an angel investor. After the lecture, I went up and introduced myself to the speaker. He said he didn't want to scare me, but he was supposed to tell me don't worry about the money and soldier on. As my shock wore off, we began to talk more about the SWF mission and his and my own personal faith. I had just finished reading a book about a felon who transformed his life and then pastored a 4,000-member church. I shared the stories in the book with the speaker and he revealed that the felon was one he had ministered to in prison. *"There's no such thing as a coincidence. It's God's way of performing a miracle and remaining anonymous."*

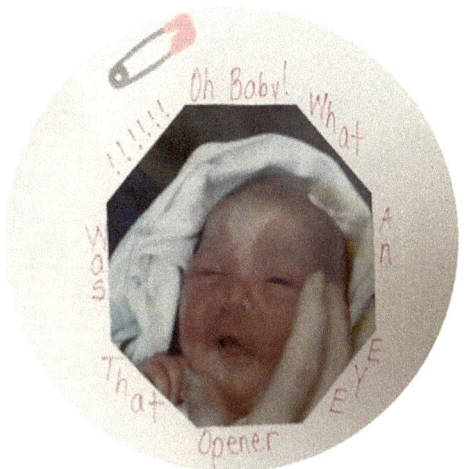

Hello world!

Another generation of a stylish maven in the making!

So proud of her first steps!

Kaelin and Karen.

I have great respect for warriors—whether they be on the battlefield, volunteering their time for a cause they believe in, or on the front lines of an emergency room. The short of it is ... I love my daughter beyond reason and knew when she was born that we would face many battles. I had better get trained and outfitted if I wanted to win the war not only for her but for those who shared her diagnosis! *The Warrior Mama* was born.

> *Hebrews 12:1-3 NIV. Therefore, since we are surrounded by such a great cloud of witnesses, let us throw off everything that hinders and the sin that so easily entangles, and let us run with perseverance the race marked out for us. Let us fix our eyes on Jesus, the author and perfector of our faith, who for the joy set before him endured the cross, scorning its shame, and sat down at the right hand of the throne of God. Consider him who endured such opposition from sinful people, so that you will not grow weary and lose heart.*

Introduction

The Fork in the Road...
or Was It the One in Our Hand?

Well, this play on words is most appropriate since our family doesn't eat to live but lives to eat and has for many generations. Irony is what keeps this life interesting, doesn't it? Let's face it, who among us hasn't hit that fork in the road when you don't know which way to go. We either have faith and leave it in God's hands or we struggle on and blame it on the fates... potentially setting oneself up to repeat the struggle or struggles. Our family has always used food to celebrate and to soothe our feelings at any given moment. So, when you hit that fork in the road... take out your fork and dig in... literally AND figuratively! On your life's journey, there's really only one way forward: just put one foot in front of the other and refuel as needed! As you will read, our family not only refueled on food but Soul food. Our Soul food are the stories of laughter and tears that are swapped around the table or any ol' time we get together. Of course, NONE of us EVER stretches the truth in the tales!

For some reason, the Holy Spirit likes to converse with me at 2:00–2:30 a.m. I wake up with words needing to be written down and hoping that they will be read and perhaps ease the path of another. I am grateful that my heavenly and earthly fathers are willing to let me share them with you. My earthly Daddy doesn't really think he's anything special... just being him, but the rest of us know differently, and now you will as well.

It took a while to really believe God was directing this publication. The trust in the rightness of writing the book took hold though, and then it just burst forth—like the words out of my mouth usually do! I've never been one to TRULY like the limelight ... now some folks will say "no, not true ... but in my core I'm bashful and would rather that others shine more brightly than me. So alas, the Good Lord had other plans which has gotten you the reader and me the scribe here today!

Most religions have doctrines they have established to frame their beliefs. Being raised in the Methodist and Baptist faiths, our family always tried to follow the dogma of these religions: "Your prayers, your presence, your gifts, and your service." This book shows how the religious beliefs were interpreted by respective Fisher/Hanley generations and how our commitment to upholding them has impacted thousands—maybe tens of thousands—of lives in the process. Again, we don't think we're any more special than the next guy, but only God knows why this book came into being out of my heart and into your hands!

MOO, B, Kaelin, and Derek atop a Montana firetower on a campout!

Introduction

MOO and B joined me at a San Diego fundraiser.

I am thankful for the opportunity that God's given me to share our story with you, which would not have been possible without the following inspirational people:

Mama and Daddy, Bev and Stan Fisher, whose faith in God and me brought me here literally and figuratively! Gramma Lou and Gramma Fisher: their faith was our families' bedrock and foundation. And our relatives who came before them, who showed my Grammas that anything worth building starts one brick of faith at a time and will create a path to heaven on earth and hereafter.

Kaelin and Derek, the world's best children! All my nieces and nephews who will carry our story in their hearts and retell it to those whose lives they touch by their prayers, presence, gifts, and service. They have all faced the proverbial forks in the road with their respective personal challenges. We all have! It's the decisions we make at the fork which directs the good, bad, and ugly that happens to us. Which doctor to choose? Which educational program and tools to use? Do I stay or go and get the divorce? Each fork in our lives needs prayerful consideration and then let it go—or, and in our family's case—whip out that fork and dive in until the answer arrives!

Finally, to you dear reader, who picked this up and maybe perused the title and turned it over to read the back cover. This book is in your hands because the good Lord wants it to be … for a reason. I hope when you are done that you've been entertained along with the reading and gained a little more insight into the reason why you needed to hear our story. I hope you feel more at peace and at the same time uplifted to bring joy and inspiration to other people as you tell your personal story and come in contact with them every day. I hope you share the book with another person in need of the telling.

All grown up!

PART I
FAMILY

CHAPTER 1

Faith and Family

... for a Reason, a Season, or a Lifetime

Blessings. I look for them in the midst of any type of storm or celebration. That desire to find grace and peace during trials has been ingrained in me all my life. My Mama and Daddy showed me by example and actions that God is always with us, and trusting in him is the only way to make it through this life. Of course, THEIR mamas and daddies showed them, and so on and so on! Being good Methodists and Baptists, the leaps of faith often involved potluck suppers and a bevy of good food. *(Karen's Two Cents: Except for the one potluck supper where my baby finger got caught in the door and we went to the ER for stitches and THEN to the potluck supper ... why spoil a good dinner?)*

Both of my parents were left fatherless at an early age. Really so not fair, but their mamas didn't have time to sit down and cry, and begging for a handout was not EVEN on the radar. The post-Depression era was hardscrabble and made harder in Montana by cold winters. Two families and two different stories—but both deeply faith-filled. They planted roots for the next generation to have it a lil' bit better than they did—and we are so thankful! I have been able to accomplish many things in this life and receive many honors, because with faith, hope, and love, giving up was never an option ... God had a plan. Sure, there were plenty of times I stumbled and sat down—more times than I care to admit—but STAYING DOWN and defeated did not honor God, my family, and most importantly

Kaelin. I know not every person has been blessed with strong family values or even a family. Those people have a tougher time in establishing and maintaining their frontline. They either have an innate internal fortitude and caring mentors or they flounder, crash, and burn. Family is so key to success and a positive sense of self-esteem, and—in tandem with grounded faith—any war can be won! I am proud to share my parents with you as two of the most influential people in my life, next to my daughter, Kaelin.

The Warrior Mama's Family

This is the most treasured section for me! I hope it will give you a little more insight as to the life foundation that enabled me to grow in faith, and also to incorporate the Sturge-Weber Foundation (SWF)—and how the SWF has survived all these years.

My dad, Stanley "Stan" Max Fisher, and my mom, Beverly Jean "Bev" Hanley Fisher, will share their memories through the years. Then, I'll share some of my recollections influenced by the generations before me. We have been blessed with a close family. If you have not had a close family and are hungering for the same, I believe you only need to look up and offer praise ... for God's presence IS all around us, and his love is profusely given. My brothers and our children have the courage of conviction and strength to shoulder on through the tough times, and celebrate with abandon the good times, because family is where our story begins!

Stanley "Stan" Max Fisher:
December 1, 1929—Stan the Man!

Born 12-01-1929 in Susanville, California. I'm told it was on the kitchen table.

My Dad was Otis Andrew Fisher and my Mom was Roberta Gatherer Fisher. Roberta's mother, Charlotte, got left by her brother (who chickened out to sail) at the dockside in Sweden at 16 years old and came to America by herself!

Charlotte Gatherer—MOO's Gramma (left); Roberta Fisher and Stan "MOO."

We moved to Willows, California around 1933—a place that was hot and had a lot of bugs. There was a revival group that came to town and they were very loud—lots of singing and organ music. Everyone was complaining, and so to be helpful I did my part: I took an ax and hacked away at the organ. *(Karen's Two Cents: Ah-haaaaaaaa! Mayhaps this is why he's never liked to sing in church!)* I came home and

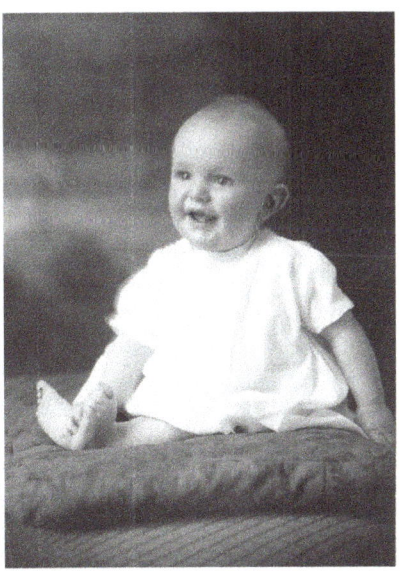

told my Mom she didn't have to worry anymore because I took care of it. I understand my father was quite embarrassed and did reimburse the group. These were hard times for everyone, because there was the Great Depression in this country during the 1930s and it was "root hog or die."

We moved to Montana in 1936. I started school in Helena at Central School. I did not like it. Mrs. Smith, my teacher in third grade, confirmed this dislike. Every night I'd pray, "Dear Lord, please let me pass third grade." I did and Mrs. Smith did too. The good Lord has a sense of humor, so I had her in the fourth grade as well.

There were five kids in the family: Truxton (Trux), Roland, then me, and then Bruce and Connie. Connie was born in 1937 and soon contracted whooping cough. She was very ill for a six- to eight-month-old baby. That year my Mom was hospitalized and had a kidney removed. While in the hospital they left the window open and she contracted pneumonia. It was touch and go for some days.

Then in October of that same year, my brother Roland was shot while bird hunting in Townsend, Montana. A Boy Scout friend had

Otis Fisher (left) and Roberta Fisher.

learned that with a gunshot wound you had to keep it moist … so went to the creek to wet a sweatshirt to put on the wound. Roland later kept telling a story that the ambulance people kept trying to put a bloody sweatshirt over his face. The hospital granted him leave for

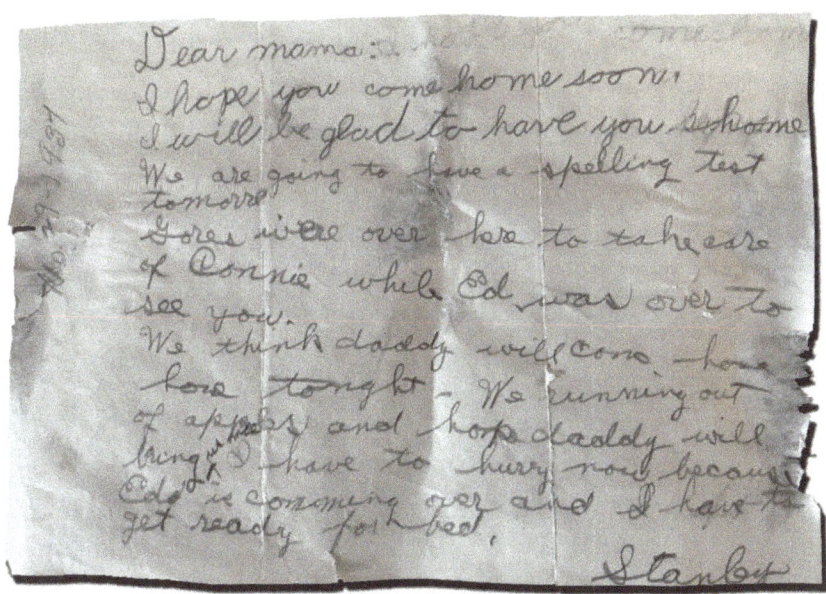

MOO: Hard-working daredevil through the years!

Christmas, but he had to go back for two more months. This too, was a very trying time for the family. *(Karen's Two Cents: With no insurance, the family paid the bill and didn't rely on others to share their burden!)*

My parents were very strict. Once when I was five or six years old, we were visiting my Aunt Edna in Asotin, Washington. I did not want to finish my morning breakfast—a bowl of oatmeal—so I was made to sit at the breakfast table from 8:00 a.m. until 11:30 and was denied lunch . . . I showed them. I then proceeded to sing "Boo Hoo (You've Got Me Crying for You)," a popular song at the time. My Mom and aunt kept trying to hide the fact they were laughing. *(Karen's Two Cents: And THIS must be why he DID like to sing lil' ditties ANY other time!)* Oh, well I guess I amused them, but I still didn't get lunch. And then they had the audacity to let me sit in the car while they went and got an ice cream. *That hurt!*

My father died on November 8, 1943. *(Karen's Two Cents: Daddy just recently told me his mom kept them out of school for one week after his dad died, and when he went back to school his teacher—who was not known to be demonstrative—walked by his desk and said "Stanley, I'm sorry to hear your dad died." She handed him a stack of homework paper and said he could take a week to finish it . . . 'course, we all know how much Daddy loved school, and he said he couldn't believe it!)* My brother Trux was in the Navy and they worked very hard to get him a leave to come home so he could be with us. He left shortly after and was stationed in the South Pacific. He returned safely in 1945.

Oh yes, one of my other tasks in the winter was to get up Sunday mornings and shovel the Baptist Church walk. Some mornings it was damn cold and it was a walk of about eight blocks to and from the church. I got to do the steps because Roland was older and bigger. We didn't have a car after my Dad died, but we all walked to church every Sunday.

In the summer, Mom cooked at the Baptist Church Camp at Templed Hills, south of Livingston. This was—as far as Mom was concerned—her vacation, and each of us kids got to go for a week. During this time, I joined the Boy Scouts and did quite well.

I worked most of my young life. I had a paper route. (I've always loved ice cream and when I'd make a nickel, I'd buy a cone.) Then, I set pins in a bowling alley—the old wooden one-pin-at-a-time hand-set kind! You had to be quick to get out of the way of the pins! I also boxed groceries at Buttrey's grocery store. I then worked in a service station until I graduated from high school. I started my first job in 1938 *(Karen's Two Cents: note that he was thirteen)* and worked all through grade school and high school.

Genevieve "Gen" was one of my paper route customers. She lived across the street from us, and after dad died and mom started to work in a donut shop—early, early mornings—Gen would always have a

Roberta and MOO (left). MOO's graduation portrait—FINALLY made it!

Gotta put food on the table! Right: MOO teaching his brother Bruce to shoot. Gotta defend the country!

cup of cocoa or something for me to eat as we talked off and on about life with the paper delivery. Gen got mom a job with the State and was always pushing me to apply to the Carter Oil Company while I politely listened. She was relentless. Finally, I went and set up an interview. I said, "I'll show her" and was told I had to interview in marketing with a Mr. Carl Yantis ... more on him later.

When I was in high school, I became a DeMolay and later (in 1951) became a Mason. I joined the Montana National Guard in 1947—Buck Private E-1. I rose to the rank of Sergeant and later in 1952 was commissioned a Second Lieutenant.

When I graduated from high school, I worked at the Montana Highway Department to save money for college. I saved $900.00 that

 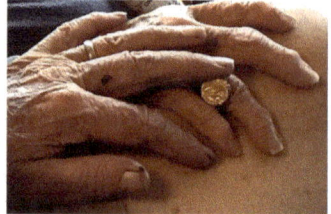

Just married! The tales these hands could tell!

Faith and Family 9

Who keeps their very first AND last paychecks?

year, which was enough for board and room my first year. I went to the Montana School of Mines in Butte. I left after one year as I was a fast learner and they didn't want me. While in school in Butte, my brother Trux got me a job on weekends working for the Anaconda Smelter.

While I was going to school, I met a girl on a blind date by the name of Beverly Hanley. She lived at 1608 North Main in Walkerville. This had to be by divine intervention, because she thought I was a kid and I thought she had to be twenty-five by the way she acted (she was twenty). It took a couple of dates to figure each other out. After I left school, I went back to the Montana Highway Department from 1950–1953. Think I wore out a car chasing to Butte to see Beverly. She learned to like me.

Cleanest Carter Station Bathroom Contest Winner! (R): Stan Stan the Travelin' Man!

Are You for Real?

Mr. Yantis wasn't there the day I was to interview at the Carter Oil Company, so after two interviews with some other men I came home. One man asked me what I wanted to do and I told him I would dig a hole one day and fill it in the next if that's what they asked me to do—but I wanted to better myself and didn't want to still be doing the same thing later on in life. The look on his face said "Buddy, are you for real?"

(Karen's Two Cents: As Daddy was telling me this story, he got that classic slow-spreading grin on his face, which he is so known for when he gets warmed up with "the tellin,'" and HIS LOOK said he didn't see anything so unusual with his comments to the fella ... and that's what makes Daddy so special ... he doesn't put on airs; he tells it like it is, and if he judges you, he never lectures— just lays it out there ... he figures we know right from wrong ... enuf said.)

I got a call later that said Carter Oil Company would like to hire you and I said "Well, I have to check with my fiancé." So, from then on, as long as Beverly didn't have to live in Helena, she was game. *(Karen's Two Cents: So, was it really ol' Gen that made the momentous changes in Daddy's family life happen, or was it that ol' adage, "There's no such thing as a coincidence; it's God's way of performing a miracle and remaining anonymous," making their life a reality and so much better for the caring. And in a further Doo-do-doo-do Doo-do-doo-do moment, Gen told Gramma Fisher that Beverly, "Bev," was pregnant, when Bev hadn't even told Gramma Fisher or known herself!)*

I went to work in Billings for Carter Oil at $280.00 a month. Big $$$s. I moved there in January 1953 and married Bev on February 15 on a five-day break from work. Too broke for a honeymoon, I went back to work on the eighteenth. All the time, however, I've been smart enough to keep my thoughts to myself. One exception: On our first time shopping after we were married, we went to a Safeway store and she picked up two pounds of butter and I said we always ate margarine, to which she replied, "*We* always ate butter." Being a quick learner and figuring married bliss was worth eighty cents (for the two pounds!), I have forever more kept my mouth shut. I loaded and drove tankers until August 1954. Gregg, our oldest was born on February 13, 1954.

We transferred to Spokane, Washington in August of '54. Karen was born January 31, 1958, and Paul December 29, 1959. I was promoted to Salesman, which turned out to be a s---y assignment due to market conditions. I retired from the National Guard in 1959 as First Lieutenant and was transferred to Miles City, Montana, as a salesman for Eastern Montana. One big territory!

While we lived in Miles City, I'd take Gregg hunting and fishing with me. We shot deer, antelope, and pheasants *(Karen's Two Cents: Daddy still knows how to make a venison steak melt in your mouth and momma has a hat she made from the pheasant tails!)* and hunted until our locker was full. It got mighty hot in the summer and as cold in the winter. One morning Bev sent Gregg off to school (he walked—no buses in those days). Later in the morning we found out it was below zero. He's a good strong kid even today. *(Karen's Two Cents: MOO had a boss named Lyle Roseberry, and his influence on MOO's personal and professional life were legend! Roseberry was a natural-born cigar smokin' and wide grinnin' salesman and risk taker.... MOO owned part of a cow herd and helped shear a herd of sheep where they thought it fine to throw lil' ol' Karen in the chute to tamp down the sheared wool, and we had many fun times at Roseberry's cabin ... like the time Daddy lifted me up and I—well, I thought—bravely stuck my finger in to feel the stuffed bobcat tongue ... it felt like pink bubble gum. It was about this time I became aware of how much my Daddy loved hunting and fishing. Their last venture was buying property together, which they bought in June—and Roseberry died that August, leaving ol' MOO to handle the mortgage payment fallout!)*

We were moved back to Billings, where I was the Company Real Estate Representative. The job was to buy service station sites in Montana, Wyoming, Idaho, and North and South Dakota. This was a real education in real estate dealing and I really liked that assignment.

Next move was to Bismarck, North Dakota as a District Manager, with responsibilities for North and South Dakota sales with a sales force of five fellas. My shining accomplishment was to win a region-wide contest (twelve states) for the cleanest restrooms. True story! Little did I realize what attention this would bring to me. In August 1966 the phone rings. I say hello and Mr. Chidsey, my boss, said congratulations. I said why? I was promoted in the region's Real Estate Department to Chicago as assistant coordinator. (So much for clean toilets).

After living in Chicago for twenty-three years (or so it seemed; it was really only eight months), we were transferred to Dallas, Texas. This turned out to be quite different than Chicago. My boss in Dallas was a stupid Irishman who had never seen the inside of a company car. Worst part—everyone thought "he hung the moon." *(Karen's Two Cents: Good news was MOO met up with ol' Mr. Carl Yantis again in Dallas, which made life easier to bear while missing Montana. And in MOO's lifelong example to all of us of looking after others, when they retired and moved to Bigfork, they kept an eye on Mrs. Yantis after Mr. Yantis died—and when she broke her hip at ninety-two—until the day she died.)* Brian, Number Three son, was born July 24, 1969—an honest to goodness Texan.

Having done my penance in Dallas for two long, long years, I received an assignment in the "mecca" for all Exxon Employees—Houston, Texas. Not only did I wonder how a stump jumper (a person from the backwoods or a redneck) from Montana with little formal education and a glib tongue could end up in Houston, but I was privileged to work for a man who was General Manager of Carter Oil when I went to work in 1953. (Carter and Exxon—all the same company.) Mr. C. D. (Colonel) Hill made all my previous sufferings go away, and being a compassionate man taught me the way of corporate politics—don't kill your adversary, but instead talk 'em to death (corporate style). He also taught me the saying, "That stuff don't stink till you stir it." He made up—management-wise—for all the bad guys I had before, and boy there were a couple. *(Karen's Two Cents:*

Fish or Cut Bait! Right: Founding Trustee, Klein UMC.

Since we had no family in any of the various cities we lived, Mama was always inviting people over to our house. The Hills used to come for Thanksgiving and Mrs. Hill made the BEST pecan pie! I watched how Daddy and Mama honored Colonel Hill and later how they took care of Mrs. Hill after the colonel passed away. As always, we've been taught by example and if there ever was an example of being a good Christian, let me tell you my Daddy DOES have the patience of a saint and Mama his best right-hand helper! There was one time when I could tell Mama 'n' Daddy were getting a lil' gritchy with each other and he was just about fed UP. He interrupted my Mama's chatter and looked at his watch. Then he looked back up and said, "Bev, what day is today?" and she said "Wednesday!" and he looked at her and calmly said, "OK, you can be the boss today!")

My job in Houston was to oversee and manage the sale of the Company's property that had been declared surplus to the company needs and get the cash for reimbursement and relieve the company of their responsibility. (SUPER JOB—held it for fourteen years) While living in Houston, I was a precinct chairman for the Republican Party, served as a Grand Jury member, and sat on the Appraisal Review Board. Bev and I were founding members of Klein United Methodist Church, and I also served on the Finance Committee and still volunteer today.

I got the name of MOO because I gave it to myself! You see, a daughter of *mine (Karen's Two Cents: That would be his one and only.)* wanted to do something "dumb" and I tol' her "No." Then, her little brother *(Karen's Two Cents: That would be the busy li'l beaver always with a retort, Paul.)* piped up and explained to me that I never let you kids

Left: Bigfork, Montana—the place where all the world's problems were solved from this viewpoint! Right: Mis Raices Estan Aqui.

do nothin' and that I was pretty narrow-minded. So, I said to "Mr. Mouth"—"I am MOO," to which he said, "What does MOO mean?" I told him, "Mighty omnipotent one," and that ended the discussion because he did not know what "omnipotent" meant and from then on I was MOO and shall forever remain such.

In 1983, I retired after thirty-one years with Exxon, sold real estate in Houston for eight years, and finally, in 1991, went to Bigfork, Montana, a place where *"Mis Raices Estan Aqui"*—"My roots are buried here."

(Karen's Two Cents: John Wayne is Daddy's idol and that saying is one of the Duke's. We have a cherished Fourth of July tradition when MOO calls and lets us listen to the Duke reciting "America, Why I Love Her." One time in front of the Alamo my brother Paul, sister-in-law Millie, and Kirk and I purchased a life-size cardboard cutout of the Duke and took a photo with the Duke and mailed them both to Dad as a joke … little did we know until the Park Ranger shooed us away that it was a no-no! MOO still has The Duke in his office!)

The Montana legislative chambers. Daddy's seat was on the left side of the aisle.

We've always been interested in local government. Some things never change.

In 1998, I ran for and was elected to the Montana House of Representatives where I served three terms (six years). It was a great experience. It is too bad more people don't get involved to understand how our government works. Not everyone that serves does so for their own need to get ahead. I'd like to think I added to the good of the State and decided six years was long enough.

Life does not just happen, but it has been directed. A person must take and act on opportunities which they are given, with the support of others. In my case, I like to think I have strong faith and act within the rules of that faith. In my case, most of my successes, whatever they might have been, came from the help and guidance from others and the faith that was picked up along the way. My Mom showed that through all the trials she endured. Unfortunately, some of the strengths each of us acquires, or develops, has come at the expense and sorrows of others. This is strange, but true. I think this says it all.

Conclusion: Best of all, through all my "fits" about the world we live in and the trials of the jobs, there was that girl who left Walkerville to train me in my shortcomings and make me believe I was a lot better than I really was. She was even better than C. D. Hill.

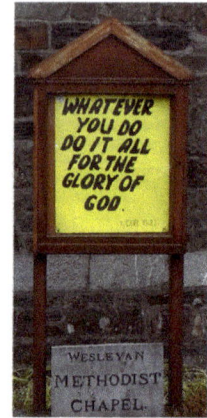

(Karen's Two Cents: Court Jester? Troubadour? Stand-Up Comedian? Whatever moniker you choose to use with this man, it has to include funny, heartfelt, and sensitive. All his life he has been the master of self-deprecation and he has perfected the art of making you at ease in his presence. Whether at work or play, he knows we do not get out of this life alive and we might as well grin and bear it in the process. He has worked, by the way, his entire life since he was thirteen years old, when he began selling newspapers for a nickel apiece.

You may be wondering about the title and after an introduction like that it is my pleasure to tell you! As with most of his best witticisms and quips, Daddy's timing is terrific and right on. My brother, Paul, is the one who has the closest propensity to be funny like Daddy and just as strong minded. Kids usually believe their parents know everything but start slipping in that belief in the teenage years. Parents typically start guiding us to follow the straight and narrow. During these same ol' teenage years, they can butt heads with "the lil' chilruns" in attempts to guide our exuberance for life. Suffice it to say the Fisher kids had lots of exuberance and Daddy has a hard head to refute those lil' "butt"-filled moments ... AND he has the patience of a saint ... usually in the form of "do it the first time every time I say so.".)

When those hands go up, you know it's gonna be a good 'un!

Daddy has always used humor and self-deprecation to make a point or ease tension in any given situation. The sly grin or stern stare that accompanies Daddy's declaration every time he has told us "because I am MOO" lets us know we are loved beyond measure but we sure as heck better believe the man is NOT gonna change his mind. It has since become his signature on letters and cards and a reminder to not take ourselves too seriously and that we are loved. Here's a typical MOO response when I showed him the first draft of this book. *"We need to talk! I ain't no saint—I just look like one. Kinda strong, but if you think so how can I argue?"* — MOO

He has always liked Will Rogers and John Wayne. He definitely believes your dog is your best friend too! In many ways, MOO really does remind me of them too. There's just a moral code he believes in and never waivers from in life. He lives that Boy Scout creed, learned in his youth, of duty to God and country, and to help other people at all times. You just always know what you are getting with Ol' Stan the Man. He's a standup guy who would never stab you in the back when you turn around; a man you are drawn to because he makes your day a little better and he puts a smile on your face just for having been in his presence.

He loves the attention if it makes you laugh or smile but at the same time does not mind the attention to be on him. I think that's what my siblings and I have also acquired from him. He taught us to ease the path of another by thought, word, and deed, and know God calls us to do whatever we can for our fellow man and have a good time while doing it.

Beverly "Bev" Jean Hanley Fisher: September 24, 1929—Stylish Maven

Beverly (Bev) has always been a "stylish maven" *(with "great gams," so says my Dad!)* and a go-getter! She had the gift of gab from an early age, and her outgoing banter and engaging personality overshadows a bashful persona. Her daddy died when she was seven years old, and her family went to live with her Uncle Gundry (aka Unk), Aunt Anne, and Ganky. Bev's a talented painter and musician, playing both violin and piano. Her sewing prowess is well-documented in the pictures of the stylish outfits she made for me over the years.

Dad died in 1937—I was seven. My Mom and Dad—Louisa Laura Hill and James Lee Hanley ("Lee")—met in Butte, Montana when they both were going to Butte Business College. Mainly, Butte was and still is an area containing a few (what today would be) suburbs, such as Walkerville and Centerville, where I grew up.

Amelia Richards Ralph (1844–1907).

Emma Ralph Hanley (1870–1951).

Peter B. Ralph "Grandpa" (1842–1908) and "Uncle" Francis Ralph.

"Ganky" Mrs. John Hill and Louisa "Lou" Hill (Hanley, Benson), c.1914.

They began married life in Centerville, which was an area about a mile north of Butte that had a mix of people—English, Irish, Italian—almost any nationality you'd want to mention. Of course, there was no "political correctness" in those days. The Irish, Italians, Jews, Yugoslavians, Polish, Hungarians, even English were called Micks, Wops, Kikes, Polacks, and many more names that today would be unacceptable. Everyone got along and was proud of their heritage. Butte was a copper-mining city and my Grampa, John Hill, ran for

coroner and was a miner, just like the majority of men. My Grampa John Hanley (whom I never knew) was also a miner. My Dad was a machinist, but not in the mines.

I was born at home with a midwife assisting in the delivery in Centerville in 1929. We soon moved to Walkerville (another city, about a couple of miles north of the center of Butte, which was incorporated). Very small population, but they had their own mayor and city council, and my Grampa Hill was Mayor and after he died my Gram became treasurer. When she died my Aunt Ann became treasurer. Absolutely no nepotism there, right? Most women when they married "stayed home" as my mom did, until my dad died.

Dad bought a house in Walkerville (near Centerville—my Mom's folks lived there; my Dad's folks in Centerville) as our family was growing. It was straight up the hill from Butte. We'd go to Centerville every Sunday after church to visit my Gramma Emmie (my Dad's Mom). She lived alone after my Grampa John Hanley died. Many years later she moved in with one of my Dad's sisters, Pearl Harrington. There were six kids in that family—my Dad, Lee, and brothers Ray, Wilbur, and Jake, plus two sisters, Pearl and Sis Ganyaw. Her real name was Amelia.

When my brother Don was born it was minus sixty degrees. My Gram—Annie Hill (Ganky to me) walked from her house, carrying a heater, to ours so we could add a little more warmth. It probably

Gramma Lou and Bev, 1929.

Louisa and Gundry "Unk" Hill. Still have the china doll. Hanley residence, 1918 (r).

was close to a mile. Don developed a few medical problems early in his life. He had a mastoid ear operation, appendix removed when he was two … and through it all eventually grew into a healthy kid. I had scarlet fever (I was probably around five at the time), and in those days sick houses were quarantined. My Dad couldn't stay at home so he'd come every night and look in the window. One night he had a special request number on the radio for me. I still remember—it was "Goodnight Sweetheart." My Ganky was always there when Mom needed any help. (*Karen's Two Cents: Ganky was a helper too! As a teenager, she babysat and changed U.S. Senator (MT) Mike Mansfield's diapers.*

It seemed like there was always, I guess you could say, a crisis in those days. When Don was four and our other brother Bruce was six months old, our Dad died. He was thirty-seven. There was never a question as to how we would carry on, it was just accepted that we'd move in with my Ganky, as well as my Uncle Gundry—"Unk" and Aunt Ann. Mom sold our house, and with a one thousand dollar insurance policy, preparations were made to add a bedroom addition to their house. We moved when it was completed. My Mom and I slept in one bed and Bruce and Don slept in a roll-away. We stayed there until I married Stan Fisher from Helena, Montana, in 1953. FAMILY was what it was all about. My Dad's brother, Wilbur, worked for the Montana Power Company, and he arranged a job for Mom.

Lee Hanley and Louisa Hill Hanley engagement photo.

During the Depression Aunt Ann and Unk lived in Troy, Montana, on a farm my Grampa John Hill bought—who knows how or when since he was, as I said, a miner in Butte. Troy is hundreds of miles from Butte and how he ever got up there I have no idea. They lived on the farm until 1935 when my Grampa died in Butte and they decided they had to move back to take care of my Gram. My Dad, who worked for the Sheep Shearers Merchandise and Commission Co., was able to get Unk a job working there as well. (FAMILY.)

My Aunt Ann was the glue holding everything together. We never considered we had a bad deal. It seemed perfect as far as we were concerned. If ever there was someone who should be considered for sainthood it was she. Don't believe even today they have saints in the Methodist Church!

Health issues seemed to plague us. My brother Bruce had a ruptured appendix when he was about four, I think. *(Karen's Two Cents: Bruce told me he floated above the surgery table and saw Unk parking the car and told them after surgery exactly where he parked it and he saw the surgeon go out for a smoke in the hall. The surgeon told him "welcome back" after he woke up . . . Doo-do-doo-do Doo-do-doo-do!)* He later developed pneumonia which led to a rheumatic heart condition. He was in bed for a long time. That led to nephritis—I guess from being inactive. He really had trouble walking because he was so weak. Then there

 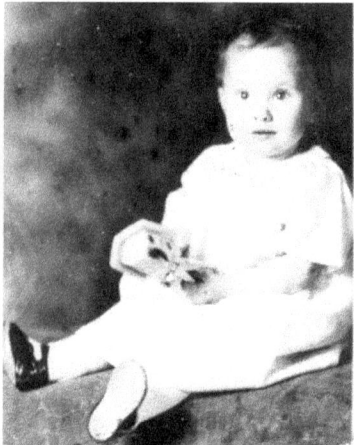 

Beverly Jean—stylish maven from the get-go!

was the time he was climbing on the fence, caught his pant leg on one of the pickets, and managed to break his arm. There was no health insurance in those days so there were always tremendous doctor bills. Doctors would come to the house, which helped when you were really sick. They'd put you to bed when you had a bad cold with a mustard plaster on your chest to break up the cough. Now you ask, what is a mustard plaster? They would take a cloth and make a paste of flour, mustard, and very hot water. Then they lay that on your chest to supposedly draw out the phlegm. We also (for colds) would be given a spoonful of baked onions, brown sugar, and butter. It tasted pretty good. Oh, yes, whiskey and honey soothed sore throats. Cod liver oil was another daily dose. Oh, how I hated swallowing that oil.

It was Aunt Ann who kept watch over all of this, along with my Ganky, as Mom worked five days a week. On weekends she was in charge.

As a kid I had regular chores. Aunt Ann taught me to iron and I felt so "big" being able to iron a shirt properly. I usually dried the dishes and on weekends got to dust. Those were my main chores, but sometimes they'd let me wash the kitchen floor and mangle the dishtowels and tablecloths. I really never thought of it as work, it was just a privilege to be able to help.

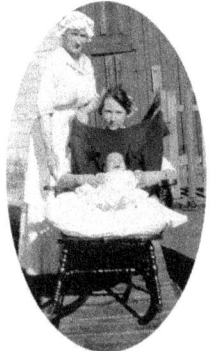  

Left: Ganky, Gramma Lou, and Bev, 1929; center: Bev still tolerates dogs to this day; right: Ganky and Bev, "stylish mavens."

My Gram, Mom, and Aunt Ann were all terrific cooks. Aunt Ann taught me to cook too and I (being Beverly) knew I could do anything. One time I got to "run" the house while Mom was at work. My Ganky, Aunt Ann, and Unk took a trip to Seattle. This was during the war years and we had a few chickens in the back yard for eggs and eventually to eat. (It saved on ration stamps.) It was summer and I decided I'd make a peach pie. I made the crust, just like I'd watched Aunt Ann make it a zillion times, and we had dinner (I don't really remember what else I'd fixed). It came time for dessert and the pie. You couldn't cut that crust with a sledge-hammer. We ate the peaches and threw the rest out for the chickens. The next morning, we looked out and one of the chickens was dead. I know it was from old age but believe me, those brothers of mine wouldn't let me live it down. *I killed the chicken with my crust,* or so they said.

One day Mom came home from work and Don went crying to her about a kid named Beavis who was always picking on him. I'm sure she was tired, but let me tell you: no one dared cross her path if she'd made up her mind to do something. *(Karen's Two Cents: FAMILY trait!)* She grabbed Don by the hand and, with Bruce and me trailing behind, marched him over to Beavis's house. She knocked on the door and asked for the kid to come out and with that told Don to fight him. After that fight, he never had any trouble with that kid.

The Mt. Bethel Methodist Church was just across the street and Aunt Ann made sure we got there every Sunday. We never missed

Gundry "Unk" Hill; right: Bev still loves to talk!

Sunrise Services on Easter and of course I always had a new dress—made by my Gram. Aunt Ann taught Sunday School and Ganky and Aunt Ann belonged to the Ladies Aid Society. This group still tends to the needs of the churches today. They would have Harvest Festivals to raise money and my Gram would lead the ladies in making pasties to sell along with other goodies. In case you have no earthly idea what a pasty (pronounced pass-tee) is, let me explain. It is meat, potatoes, and onions encased in a very rich pie crust. I never got to help with the crust (I wonder why?) but they did let me peel the potatoes and set the tables for dinner. *(Karen's Two Cents: Today, my momma's flaky piecrust is as close to a bite of heaven as you can get on this side . . . just goes to show practice makes perfect!)* I think the pasties sold for about fifty cents and I'm sure they didn't charge too much for the dinners either.

My Ganky made the best pasties of anyone and she'd make them for the miners at the Lexington Mine in Walkerville. She'd make a tremendous number, and the night before she assembled them we'd cut potatoes, onions, and the meat. Then, she would cook them in the morning so they would be ready for one of them to pick them up for their lunch and I think she sold them for fifty cents. Cooperation was always what we did. Whatever needed to be done we just all pitched in. She also baked them for the teachers as well. They would let me leave school early so I could go home, get the pasties, and bring them back for their lunch. Then, of course, I had to turn around and walk back home for my lunch. Maybe that's why we were all thin—lots of walking kept us healthy. As I got older, Mt. Bethel closed due to limited attendance and we would walk about a mile to Centerville to the Trinity Methodist Church, where I always sang soprano in the choir.

There was a distant cousin who also went to church and he would entice us girls to the stairway leading from the basement (where the dinners were served) and expose himself. Now you have to remember we were maybe ten or eleven at the time. Some of us had brothers so it was no big deal but there were a few girls who didn't. I wonder what was going through their minds.

In 1942, we had an addition to our family. Aunt Ann and Unk had a baby boy, Robert. What fun we all had! Bathing, feeding, taking him for walks in his buggy—he was just like another brother.

Remember me saying how we added the bedroom addition to the house? There was one bedroom, where Aunt Ann and Unk slept, along with Robert. My Gram slept on a sofa bed in the living room and we were upstairs. It seemed right to us. Now of course, my Gram couldn't go to bed if there was any company and when Mom started dating Vern Benson (my stepdad)—who also worked for the Montana Power—they sat in the kitchen so they could be alone and Ganky could go to bed. Can you see that happening today?

We all thought we had the perfect living arrangements and none of us were too happy when she began living a life. She bowled on a team that Vern belonged to, and for too many years continued to "go along to get along." It was rather complicated. Vern lived with his sister Hilda, who was a geometry teacher, and I was always holding my breath that I didn't get her as my teacher—don't think she probably wanted me either. Only after I married did Mom and Vern get married as well. They lived in the Benson home in Butte. Hilda lived there as well. Bruce moved with Mom as he finished high school. Don was in college. Hilda never married, and there just never was a thought to her living anywhere else. (FAMILY.)

While my Dad was still living, naturally I never wanted for a thing. Rabbit fur coat, white leather gloves. My Grampa Hill would

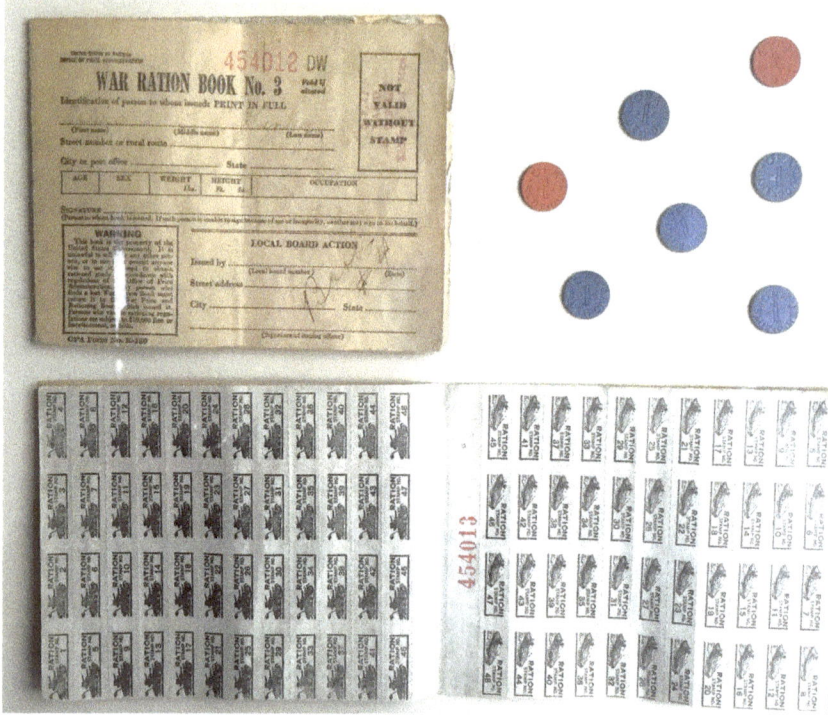

get on the street car, at the top of Main Street—by their house—and Mom would take me out to the stop by our house, which was on Daly and probably, as I said before, about a mile in distance, and he'd take me to town. We always went to Clinton's drugstore and bought butter scotches and humbugs (molasses tasting) candy. I loved it.

I started kindergarten and was bored to tears and told them I wasn't going. First grade came along and I loved school. It was always very easy for me so as I got in fourth, fifth, and through the eighth grades I got to "help" the teachers. I corrected papers and got to go to the library when I was finished with whatever we were doing. Today I believe they'd call that a teacher's pet. Maybe! There was also a tall girl named Betty. School was very hard for her and she REALLY disliked me. You couldn't fight on the school grounds but walking home for lunch she was always ready for a fight (fist kind). I did manage to give her a bloody nose one day. Just like Don, I too never had any more trouble.

I did get into plenty (of trouble, that is). One day, when we still lived in "our house" on Daly Street where I was born, my friend Shirley, whose family lived behind the Mt. Bethel Church (and who always dared me) and I went up to Ganky's house and I rifled Ganky's dresser looking for money so we could buy some candy while the ladies were playing bridge and so I thought she didn't catch me in the act! I went home after I bought the candy at Manza's Market and Mom asked where I'd been. (I used to lie quite a bit.) Whatever I'd told my mom didn't fit because my Gram had called Mom and told her what I did. I also used to get spanked a lot. I WAS a willful child. *(Karen's Two Cents: she's a willful adult too ... FAMILY trait!)*

That ol' Lord must have been keeping pretty close tabs because I never got into any serious trouble. I just knew if I did, retribution would be swift. I also knew there would always be somebody bigger than me to "bring me down a peg." While my Dad was still alive, we were going to go camping by some river. Next door to us (in our house on Daly) was an Irish family with quite a few kids. One of the girls really didn't like me (I must have been a brat) and for some reason or other dropped a huge boulder on my foot. It was indeed painful and I was not a "happy camper" that whole weekend. *(Karen's Two Cents: Perhaps this is where her loathing of picnics first surfaced?)* I bet I made it most enjoyable for everyone else, too. One of their boys was one of Don's lifelong friends. Don always did know how to get along.

I started violin lessons when I was very young—probably five or six. I hated to practice and one day Mom came home from work when I was supposed to be practicing but was just fooling around. She came in the living room, took the violin out of my hand and "bopped" me on the head. *Wrong thing to do*—it cracked the violin. She had a cousin who lived across the street from us who had a violin and gave it to me. I did practice after that and became the first violinist in the Butte High School orchestra. I used to play for a lot of churches and for Easter Sunrise services. The Latter-Day Saints church invited me often and I especially enjoyed playing there because music was such a large part of their worship service.

Vern developed Parkinson's disease after he and mom were married. Mom continued to work even after he was unable to get around. A cousin of Mom's was his caregiver (FAMILY) until he passed away. Again, Mom's quiet strength just never flagged. I guess we just always saw the glass as half full. My Aunt Ann developed breast cancer and Mom was always there for her—changing bandages and helping her as she weakened. After she died, my Unk moved closer to where Mom and Vern were. She then tended to his needs as well. (FAMILY.) We used to say Grace for special meals and did say our prayers at night but sitting reading the Bible was never a part of everyday life. Church was what we did on Sunday. Somehow, you unknowingly knew you were expected to "do the right thing," as the Good Book says, by deeds and caring for each other. We certainly learned this by example.

As kids we never fought and with the extended family, we all got along. There was just a lot of love, always. Our kids never had many disagreements and we all just love getting together as often as we can—all seventeen of us. There are nine grandkids and two great grandkids—all so special. We are so fortunate to be surrounded by such love. The grandkids are a work in progress, from Brian and Stephanie's daughter, Alexandra (who was always like seven going on twenty) and sons Blake and Grant; to Paul and Millie's four, Audrey (now married to Kevin Lenz and with two boys of her own, Nolan and Cole), Shane and Cody (now graduated and working), and Emily, who married Mac James, a baseball player (and who have a son, Elijah); to Karen and Kirk's two—Kaelin, a graduate of York College in Pennsylvania with a Master's degree, and Derek, living at the Lighthouse Christian Home in Kalispell, Montana.

It's Ten O'Clock . . . Do You Know Where Your Children Are?

(Karen's Two Cents: That saying was played on TV every night at 10:00 p.m. when I was growing up.)

High school was always easy and fun. Now remember that I was a Methodist but I ran around with kids from the Presbyterian Church and on Sunday evening we'd go to CE (Christian Endeavor) meetings. We'd go out to the Red Rooster restaurant after the meeting was over. I was always the first one to be dropped off after we'd go to the Red Rooster because I lived the furthest away. We were probably

Bev, her mom Louisa, Ganky, and Robert Hill.

seventeen years old but no one ever asked if we were of legal age and we always ordered a mixed drink. Of course, it would be just one, but on weekends when there were football or basketball games there would be beer-busts. Nothing changes, does it? I never liked beer but I always went. Oh, yes, on Friday nights we'd have "mixers" (dances actually with a band). The mixer was over at midnight so it would be 2:00 a.m. before I had to be home. We just never did get into any trouble. *(Karen's Two Cents: Maybe the broken violin over the head finally cured her of that love of trouble?)* Life would not have been worth living, let me tell you, if we did.

When I graduated from high school I was going to "just work a year" before I went to college. I just never got there. I liked making money. I became a bookkeeper at Whites Funeral Home. I took all scientific courses in high school but I certainly knew how to add and subtract. How hard could it be? The gal that had the job moved to a different funeral home and the first month I had to do a balance sheet I had no more idea how to do it than the man in the moon. I went over on my lunch hour so she could show me how. It never EVER entered my head I couldn't do something. Along with that job, I also kept books for a floral shop and a dress store. Guess where my money went?

Beverly Jean Hanley Butte Bride of Stanley Max Fisher

Miss Beverly Jean Hanley of Butte and Stanley Max Fisher were married recently in the Mountain View Methodist church in Butte. The R.v. H. L. Robertson performed the ceremony.

The altar was decorated with white candles and standards of white gladioli and stock. Mrs Roland Stanley sang "Oh Perfect Love" and "I Love Thee" accompanied by William Johns who also played a program of nuptial music on the organ.

The bride was given in marriage by her uncle, Gundry Hill. She wore a gown of ivory satin with full length train. Her long veil was caught to the head with a halo cap of seed pearls. She carried a bouquet of white orchids and stephanotis.

Miss Mary Lou Thomas, maid of honor, wore an apricot-colored dress. Mrs. Fred Angove, matron of honor was dressed in canary yellow and Miss Erma Chabai, bridesmaid wore olive green. Their bouquets and head dresses were of Talisman roses.

Flower girl, Diane Farrell of Los Angeles wore an ice pink frock trimmed with fuchsia and carried a basket of sweetheart roses.

Bruce Fisher was his brother's best man and brothers of the bride and bridegroom, Truxton Fisher of Anaconda, Roland Fisher of Great Falls, Donald L. Hanley and Bruce Hanley, ushered.

Immediately after the ceremony a reception was held at the Fez. Mrs. Hanley was assisted in entertaining by Miss Joan Corette, Mrs. George Huddleston, Miss Donna Horton and Miss Betty Birmingham. About 150 guests attended.

The table was decorated with a wedding cake surrounded with white daisies and pink roses.

On their return from a short wedding trip the couple will make their home in Billings. For traveling Mrs. Fisher chose a dusty mauve suit with brown accessories and a corsage of white orchids.

The bride is the daughter of Mrs. Louisa Hanley of Butte. She is a graduate of Butte high school.

The groom is the son of Mrs. Roberta Fisher of Helena. He was graduated from Helena high school, attended Montana School of Mines and is employed by the Carter Oil company.

I went on a blind date with this fella from the School of Mines in Butte. He called, with urging from my girlfriend Irma's boyfriend. I told him I never took blind dates. He informed me it would be okay because he wasn't blind. Right then I should have known! He asked to talk to my Mom and informed her he really was a good guy and that everyone liked him. Well, a few years later and a lot of miles between Helena (where he lived) and Butte, we did get married in 1953. I didn't particularly want to live in Helena so I kept dragging my feet, but lo and behold he got a job with Carter Oil (Exxon) and we moved to Billings, Montana. We didn't have a honeymoon because he had to get to work and I had a home to make. It never occurred to me to whine about what I didn't have, like many kids today do. We went grocery shopping and of course Stan told you his take on that trip! We also needed furniture for the home so I went and bought some on credit *(Karen's Two Cents: First time he ever*

Ganky, Gramma Lou, Bev, and son #1, Gregg.

used credit.) at a very stylish furniture store. He wasn't too happy but we did use that couch for a very long time!

How times have changed—when I was pregnant with our first child, Gregg,

Mama and me doing what I love best and she doesn't!

my Ganky sent down a gallon of Chianti wine for me to have every day to increase my blood count. I was always anemic and as a kid ate liver in almost everything, along with red wine. Guess it worked. Gregg was a healthy baby. Smart kid; he walked at eight months. We were transferred to Spokane, Washington and had our next two kids, Karen and Paul. Karen took a long time to be born and Paul was a preemie who I rocked through the night.

I love baseball. Basketball and football too, but one evening we had tickets to see the Dodgers play our farm team, the Spokane Indians. We had a babysitter and Stan and I were going into town for the game (we lived in Opportunity, which was a few miles from the center of town). I hear this crying as I was getting ready. One of the kids had climbed a pine tree *(Karen's Two Cents: Bet it was Paul!)* and fell. It was a pretty good fall and we checked him over and he seemed all right. There was some discussion of a possible concussion but it couldn't have been. Fortunately, we went to the game. Worry doesn't get you anywhere and I just knew that ol' Lord wouldn't let anything serious happen. He didn't. I loved the game. Do you think that was selfish of me? *(Karen's Two Cents: In all my years of hearing their stories this is a first!)*

We moved from there to Miles City, Montana. I always thought moving was a ball—having the opportunity to meet new people, to have new places to visit, a chance to decorate. I always got us involved in the local church and volunteered at the Red Cross and enjoyed sewing curtains, upholstering furniture, or anything to make our new homes feel homey. As I was a stay-at-home mom, it also helped us save money. Incidentally, I do love to have a change in appearances.

Ganky, Gregg, Gramma Lou, Karen, and Bev.

Our children were precocious. As is my usual practice, I always make the bed when I get up. One morning Gregg came running in and said, "Come quick!" One of them had been in the cupboard and found packets of baby aspirin. *(Karen's Two Cents: Wasn't that nice she didn't say or remember it was her food lovin' daughter, but those orange aspirins courtesy of our dentist sure were tasty too!)* Paul, the youngest, was ingesting them as if they were candy. *(Karen's Two Cents: ... and Karen was hiding the wrappers as fast as she could under her pillow ... hmmm ... early signs of hiding the guilt and evidence!)* Fortunately, we were about a block from the hospital. I got to hold his legs while the doctor pumped his stomach. There were no after-effects, but not only did I get a stern lecture on keeping medicine out of reach of the children, it was also reported to the poison control center. Very humiliating! Stan didn't have to hear the poison control report part; he was home with Gregg. *(Karen's Two Cents: Daddy never did nor still does to this day like hospitals, but is always the first one to visit a sick friend when they are admitted!)*

We then transferred to Bismarck, North Dakota, for three years. I have always volunteered and became quite involved with a nursing/retirement home. I had one couple that was so lovable. She'd always want me to pluck the stray hairs on her chin. I think of her every time I pluck one of mine. I learned quilting from her and to this day I still have the patterns that she cut out for me. *(Karen's Two Cents: I cherish the hand-stitched quilt made from all the fabric scraps of dresses Mama made me!)* When Stan had to travel for business and I could go along, we had a wonderful babysitter named Mrs. Luthlie. She would fill the freezer with the most delicious kuchens and the house was immaculate. *(Karen's Two Cents: This was also the town where Gregg and I walked home from school in a blizzard with me holding onto Gregg's coat so I wouldn't lose sight of him!)* Mrs. Bjornson was Karen's teacher and her son Daryl worked with Stan.

We then moved to Chicago and were there such a short time—like one big vacation! I loved going into the city (we lived in the western suburbs—Clarendon Hills; Stan's office was in Oakbrook).

We got tickets to see "The Nutcracker" at McCormick Center. What a wonderful evening. The next morning, we read in the paper where the Center had burned to the ground. God seems to have a hand in everything, doesn't He? Fortunately, no one was hurt and through His Grace we were rewarded. That fire could have started when we were there.

There were always baseball games, the Field Museum, and the theater. *(Karen's Two Cents: Mama has always been fearless! Driving in inner-city Chicago one time, unbeknownst to us she'd gotten lost in the housing projects with broken out windows; she used that to distract us and said to get an education and save your money!)* Another time we were going into the city to see a play. I was at the beauty shop and Stan was still at work. The kids were home and all of a sudden the sky turned black. I was anxious to get home because I was concerned they may have been frightened. As I went home (only a few blocks) there was debris all over. Turns out a tornado had ripped through the area. Going into the city it was devastating to see. Great play though. *(Karen's Two Cents: I was babysitting at ten years old for a lil' baby down the street and who wouldn't stop crying ... gee wonder why with a tornado coming! That comment is also one of the zillion reasons I love my Mama ... optimism and first things first!)* While we were there (all in the span of eight

She surely is and WILL be an angel!

Still talking! Right: Gives as good as she gets!

months), THE major snowfall hit. Everything was shut down. It was beautiful. There must have been something in God's plan to warrant such a storm. It surely brought families together. They couldn't go anyplace. Togetherness is a great thing.

To show you what a short time we were there, I became pregnant in Bismarck with our last son, Brian. He was born in Dallas, Texas, which was our next move. We had wonderful neighbors who baby-sat and still think he's a pretty cool kid. Paul was in second grade at that time. He started in Bismarck, had a real "old" teacher (very short-tempered) in Chicago who intimidated him greatly. One of these Dallas neighbors had a son with reading problems and so we commiserated. It turned out, after much doctoring, that Paul was diagnosed with dyslexia. He went to a school for Specific Learning Disabilities for one year. He questioned why he had to go there, and his Dad told him because he had trouble with learning to read and we were trying to fix it, just like we would if he had a broken arm. It never amazes me how that ol' Lord puts people in your path to help you with the next situation. I started to say problem, but as usual it only becomes a problem if you let it. *(Karen's Two Cents: And that is the outlook that has enabled my brothers and me to laugh in the face of adversity ... no problems, only challenges and opportunities!)*

We were transferred to Houston, Texas, and as I said I have always volunteered. Because of Paul's situation, we settled in an area that was north of the city—Spring. The schools were good but no one really knew how to teach children with a problem like dyslexia. I helped start a reading program, as well as an art appreciation series. One of the teachers went to a summer school to be trained in helping kids with learning disabilities. What a tremendous help that was. She never sees us that she doesn't say how appreciative she was to have been able to understand how to proceed with teaching kids like Paul.

When we first moved to Spring, we went to a Methodist church which included two or three different school districts. Since Gregg was in high school in Klein, we decided there was a need for a Methodist Church in our area to nurture our kids. Along with four other families, we started Klein Methodist Church. I taught Sunday School and sang in the choir, and we carried the altar and candles in the car trunk when we were first in the high school cafeteria. Thirty years later when we visit (at least once a year), we are amazed. Now there are thousands who attend Klein United Methodist Church. From a quote by the minister today: Jesus said, "No procrastination. No backward looks. You can't put God's kingdom off till tomorrow. Seize the day. (Luke 9:62)". I'm not really sure Jesus had a scrapbook or a yearbook of memories because Jesus' ministry has always had that forward look that beckons us to grab hold and to charge ahead wherever God leads us.

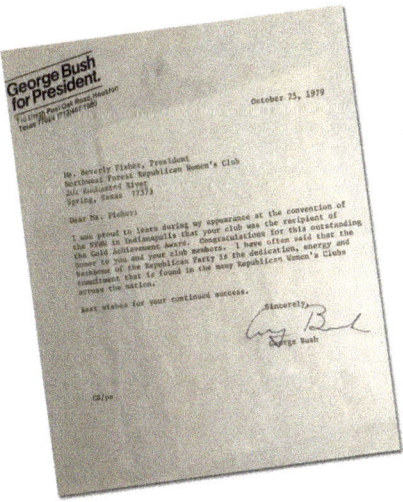

Not a bad way to end this "epistle." After all, it's the only sure thing we can count on. Yesterday is gone. Today is fleeting. Tomorrow is our greatest hope.

From the time I "pushed" election cards for my Grampa, going door to door encouraging people to vote for him, I have always loved politics. Along with the school activities I worked closely with the Republican Party. At the time we moved to the South, Republicans were heard of but there were very few in Texas. Oh, yes, we did have John Tower in the U.S. Senate. I volunteered a lot. We started a Women's Republican Club in Spring and I managed a successful campaign for the first woman judge, Pat Lykos, in Houston.

I later became Vice-Chairman for the Harris County Republican Party. The women I volunteered with and shared the joys and trials of raising children in the 1970s are still cherished friends today. Stan said I wore out three cars, but it really was worth it. *(Karen's Two Cents: She even won Woman of the Year and received a hand-typed and signed note from President George H.W. Bush!)*

Left: Best friends, family, and travel companions! Right: Ninety-one years old with her white knights, brothers Don and Bruce, beside her still. Good thing we're made of tough stock after all that life she's lived!

Egypt. Of course, she wouldn't miss the camel ride if she kissed the Blarney stone in Ireland! Paris was never the same after our cab rides and visit!

One day a fella running for a Justice of the Peace office called and asked me if I could recommend someone to run his office. Now mind you—I did a lot of volunteering, as

well as playing violin in Houston Symphony North, but I never worked outside the home. He told me the salary, which was a lot and suddenly I decided maybe it was time for me to go back to fruitful labor. I told him I would seriously consider it myself and I would commit for at least two years. It was a great job. I stepped down from the County Party and worked until Brian was out of College and we decided it was time to "come home." Stan missed the mountains.

Time marches on.

Oh yes—we did too. We now live in Bigfork, Montana, where golfing is good, and hiking, fishing, and hunting is too. I still volunteer at the Art Center and the Glacier Symphony (I don't play anymore but so enjoy being around the music). I continued to sing in church choirs and was on the finance committee at our church. That bookkeeping comes in handy! In a reversal of political roles, I became the Campaign Manager for Stan on the day he came home and said he decided to run for the Montana legislature because he had $15 in his pocket to file!

Much later in life a minister friend of ours asked how we programmed our lives. Dad and I just laughed because we all know—that plan is already in place; all you do is wake each morning, say thank you Lord, and wade in. Worry gets you no place— doesn't change a thing. There is a reason for everything, we just don't know why until we're tested. *(Karen's Two Cents: They did LOTS of traveling too! What a wonderful life they lived and live!)*

"True story!"

"So Stan, where are we going today?"

CHAPTER 2

Whispers and Imprints on My Heart

Hello! Yes, I'm Calling You!

I suppose I first heard "the call" when I was around ten years old. I recall waking up and seeing Jesus at the foot of my bed. I used to question if it was a dream but after having several more moments when visions or coincidences happened, I know he was there. It was a great comfort and a moment more like, "Oh, you really are there and peaceful and ok I'll go back to sleep now." Never thought anymore of it as the years went on and while I went to church, sang in the choir, attended youth groups, and volunteered for Vacation Bible school.

I have tried to find the same peace and feeling of safety and comfort like I felt that night through other people or places or self-abusing activities. Nothing new there since it has happened to many before and probably will after me too. Silly me though.... Wisdom does come with age, eh! I have always admired my sister-in-law Stephanie and brother Brian for teaching Sunday school and shepherding children to know Jesus IS there for them and their personal savior. They've lived their lives with a servant's heart, raising three kids close in age, all while traveling and working! It does seem misguided and smacking of lack of faith to hesitate or fight it when He calls us for good ... especially considering how *very* good that good is and how many lives are transformed by it!

Are you a morning person? I usually wake up with that "look like she got run over by a Mack truck" stare. Truth be told, without my Daddy's creative wake up calls (i.e., flipping the lights on and off, water sprinkles on the sheets, his cheerful "Good morning to you ... good morning to you song") and my Mama's slow loving caresses, I would have always been late for school and life! I am slightly more "up and at 'em" now. Those 2:00 a.m. "Helllllooo, I'm calling you" whispers the Holy Spirit sends my way does make it necessary for an extra cup of coffee though!

In high school, I did hear God calling me to trust my first boyfriend but was too scared to really trust in that relationship and the Baptist faith he was leaning on. Another boyfriend, another denomination later ... his church prayed over me in tongues and *that* was an experience! I was searching for that peace and personal one-on-one relationship with God, especially throughout high school. I was a good Methodist. However, you didn't raise your hands in praise during *that* service! I have the best Mama who let me try different churches on to see if they fit ... secretly hoping, I'm sure, that I'd regain my senses.

When my girlfriends were in a horrific car crash, I saw the power of prayer as we all prayed incessantly for our girlfriend Kathy to be brought back to life and out of her coma. My Mama urged me to pray and let me talk and talk and cry and talk about "Why, why, why did this happen?" We had many esoteric discussions of how God works in peoples' lives. I had a glimmer of "Hey, this prayer thing might really work." I had the mindset ... crisis over ... me too, as sometimes happens! I didn't pray on a daily basis and lapsed into self-absorption for many years.

Then, in college, at Baylor University as I majored in education, I shut God out until my junior year. I partied too much but alas it's what got me here today ... God, not the parties!

I have always had these "feelings" about various people and things in life. I am getting better about realizing that they sure enough better be listened to, because there is a reason—and usually not a good one. I do find it strange that I'm more often than not called to check in on someone or write something only when there's a challenge or crisis. Yet another fork in the road happened when I told my dad and mom I was going to join *Up with People* (*UWP*) after my sophomore year. It just felt like it was something I had to do, unlike the typical "feelings." There wouldn't be peace until I did. I knew I wasn't really happy doing the usual college antics mixed with studying. I even took on a job at the local Waco Albertson's (which at that time I thought beneath me) to raise money for the yearlong commitment ... my, my, my the Lord does work in mysterious ways, doesn't he!

I went for a whole year without partying which, trust me, at that time *was* a miracle! You and I know God works in mysterious ways and that was one of His finer moments! Anyway, *UWP* was a turning point in my life. I recall most vividly being in Europe and doing a mini show, as we always did before the big performances, at a private home for children with developmental disabilities and another time at a large dorm-like home for children with cerebral palsy. They profoundly affected me because I was very uncomfortable with disabled children. I just didn't know how to relate and God forbid I should have one. Yes, ma'am, that ol' Lord *does* prepare our path!

The shows were His way of opening a window. I know that now. I could "act" all happy and hold their hands while I swayed to the music ... believe I was doing something noble and good, but inwardly afraid to be with them. All along, every person, place, and situation I have met or situation I've been in led me to answer His ultimate call.

This is a book about how faith and God's loving hand in tandem with the Holy Spirit have shaped generations of Fisher and Hanley families to endure the hardships and celebrate the joys in our lives. I always knew God was there for me by watching my elder's faith and service by example. Gramma Fisher and Gramma Lou had amazing faith and proclaimed that faith with their prayers, presence, gifts, and service. They had a personal quiet faith. This book is really because of them and their influence on my Mama and Daddy, which ultimately led to their gift of faith for us.

I took another fork in the road in my thirties from quiet personal faith to sing His praises to anyone else who would listen. I *love* to tell the stories of how God has worked in my life, "nudged" me in a certain direction, or brought peace amidst a crisis. God's stories are always told with a hopefully self-deprecating and "oh, you'll never believe what happened *this* time" delivery!

To Tell or Not to Tell?

Our experiences with God are of a personal nature for a reason. Some of us are more comfortable sitting in that pew on Sunday mornings, hearing the sermon and chit-chatting with the congregation or synagogue before heading home. Some of us *love* to shout His praises to the mountaintops and wear it on our sleeves. Some of us find God early on in life or after tragic crises or addictions bring us to our knees. Let's face it: however we find Him, or as some would say, "allow Him to be heard," we are never the same and are always here to do His will.

We were always taught it's not right to be a "thumper" (rude to say I know, but as kids we always called the folks who tout scripture verse after verse and have a self-righteous demeanor by this term). We were taught faith should be lived through "actions speak louder than words." We talked about God, but it was more my Mama dragging us to church and by God "you *will* believe if it kills you" kind of mothering! Thank God she did, and He has blessed us many times over.

There was always a deep faith welling up inside me and I chuckle while writing this part of the book. I am sure my telling and telling and *tellllIng* used to wear on my Daddy's nerves. Of course, I wasn't the only one who was verbose in our family! My older brother, Gregg, really is the only quiet one. My younger brother, Paul, was more hyper than I was, and that boy could—and still can—tell a tale like no one else! Later, our baby brother, Brian, came along and he was influenced by my eloquence and Mama would say not in a good way! But I digress. By "tell" I mean to share with people a happy spirit that sees the joy in life and they should/could have joy in their life, too. The two boys and I still do engage folks we meet and can get them to smile with a bullcorn or two! Back then I was unaware that the incessant talking we were known for was really Attention Deficit Hyperactivity Disorder (ADHD). Of course, we would like to believe ADHD isn't an excuse because deep down we know what we said we *had* to be said, because the joy was so great inside us we'd burst if not said out loud. We also knew and still know maybe the person we were talking with might be a little happier or lighter for the conversation ... which usually they were! Today, I try to warn people to bring along an oxygen tank because we *can* tend to suck the oxygen right out of the joyous atmosphere!!

I *love* to tell people about how the Holy Spirit whispers and when I listen and act upon them, amazing things happen for good—and they can for you too! God *is* real and He has worked in my life in many ways. I recently was discussing with a dear friend about a feeling I had to make some changes in my life and how I talk to "the Big Guy" (aka God ... sometimes people are more receptive to the "God Talk" when the conversation is infused with humor, although my friend Maggie says it's not right to call him "the Big Guy"). My friend said he only talks to God in time of crisis like "I promise I won't do that again." I think that's pretty typical in today's hurried world, but really talking with Him all the time makes for less stressful days and clarifies our direction in life. My friend called me up later that day after he said he tried prayer before a big meeting but that I must have been talking to God or monopolized the line because he got a busy signal! It *did* make me chuckle, but I told him to keep trying and I'd put in a word for him anyway. It's becoming second nature for me to be in communion with God, but obviously there was a lotta mileage on that road to accept what His calling for me has been.

I have officially taken that fork in the road where actions speak louder than words and have found peace that blends both worlds where it's ok to do the telling along with the action!

Gramma Fisher was always "studying up with the Good Book," as my Daddy says. She found solace and courage to face the challenges life had for her! Gramma raised five kids after her husband died. With penicillin expensive, no health insurance, and being thrust into the work force to keep food on the table, no wonder she was seeking some peace *some* place! The church was their social life and her salvation, I suspect. One of my most cherished possessions is Gramma Fisher's beloved Bible, which my Daddy unselfishly gave me during a very, *very* low point in my life. Only a father with great love would sacrifice that cherished book and faith reminder! Gramma Fisher also was a member of the Eastern Star, and like all the Fisher's and Hanley's, served others all her life!

My Gramma Lou on the other hand was more social and her faith was witnessed in action. She was full of action and always on the go ... hmmm ... family trait, I do believe! She loved being in the middle of all the action and even more so

If ya gotta travel the road, carry a lunch sack and the Good Book! Gramma Fisher studied Mathew, Mark, Luke, and John so much that she had to tape the edges!

directing it. My Gramma Lou's mama, Annie Hill (or Ganky as we called her), even started a Methodist Episcopal Church in Walkerville, Montana. I have a gorgeous carved filigree frame with the certificate and sample of the robe material hanging in our home. One of my most cherished possessions of Gramma Lou's is one of those plastic pins with her name on it that says at the bottom "Volunteer."

My family has always been givers, doers, and goers. Early memories of both of them involve laughter, food, and books. Gramma Fisher loved her picnics! We'd fill up our packs and head out to the Gates of the Mountain whenever we went on vacation to see her. Her cooking style was good old fashioned homestyle: gravies, biscuits, venison, etc. Gramma Lou, on the other hand, loved to pull out the linens, china, and silver. She always set a beautiful table and the food was out of this world. If I could have filled a backpack with either one of their bills of fare, it would have been a traveling feast for the soul; that's for sure!

Put a Nickel in the Drum and You'll Be Saved!

We were always taught by example to honor our family and religion with "your prayers, your presence, your gifts, and your service." Of course, we were taught to say Grace at meals and the Lord's Prayer at night. The traditions bring comfort through the rituals and knowing where I come from keeps me grounded. We were

present in church almost every Sunday and attended the usual potluck suppers (live to eat, and do we ever!) and various concerts during all the traditional church seasons. We also got a quarter to put on the plate as it was passed around so our gift could be counted.

My Daddy also used to sing a little ditty, "Put a nickel in the drum and you'll be saved" while swinging his index finger in time to the tune. It always made us laugh because he looked so serious while being so comical. Our family has always performed community and church service. We were expected to try to make someone's path easier if there was a need. These cherished memories serve as the early bedrock leading to my lifetime of service.

The first ten years of my life were pretty much not putting any prolonged thought into who was really in charge! Typical kid, I think. I was more interested in the potluck suppers and what was for dessert … some things never change! I recall one potluck that we were headed to when I was young—maybe four or five years old. I'm sure my Mama was frazzled trying to get three kids ready to go, get the food, get dressed, and the usual routine. In our haste to make it on time, my baby finger somehow got caught in the right passenger car door. All I recall now is the door shutting, the hospital stitching up my finger and bandaging it. The other memory of that event was me sitting at the table during the potluck supper and for once she let me have an extra dessert! Now that I must say is service!

It makes me wonder now at the sheer strength of will my Mama has always had when it comes to duty. I am also in awe of the fortitude she has had all her life, which by now you know has been passed down by example. Another memory of this time was more fashion-related: we were always dressed up, out of respect for the church, as a reflection on the family, and in any situation where we only get one chance to make a first impression! My Mama is the best seamstress in the world! All my clothes except some jeans and a few shirts were made by hand, and all my prom and formal wear. I *loved* it as I never looked like anyone else in the room. Mama on the other hand most likely didn't love it all that much because she always had to adjust patterns for pants to make the waist smaller and hiney area larger.

The weight battle I'd had in early childhood wasn't so bad entering my teen years. I mean really: Was it *my* fault that they were all such good cooks? How could I *not* have a weight problem when all we think about is food and we were blessed with fantastic cooks? What to have for dinner? What to have for the weekend? That birthday? That celebration? That sad time? Etc., etc., etc.... I found a

Connie and Sybil still make me laugh today!

close-knit group of girlfriends at the bus stop, though, who pulled me out of my shyness and into activities surrounding the drill team. Guess what? The weight came down! This time of my life was fabulous between swim team, tennis team, and drill team camp during the summer and dancing during the year; I did have a nice lil' body for me! Of course, I was still tall and large compared to the socialites in the making with the petite size two body types. These were really years of personal and emotional growth.

As I mentioned earlier, Mama encouraged me to explore faith within our home, our church, the Bible and even other denominations such as Baptist and non-denominational. Does make you wonder though what she *really* thought after that time at my boyfriend's non-denominational church when they prayed over me in tongues. Remember, we have generations of ingrained belief ... actions speak louder than words ... so it must have been interesting listening to me banter about some of my experiences especially since those talking tongues were pretty loud! I look back now and of course am more informed on the whole issue of speaking in tongues. It was of course a pivotal moment that planted the seeds that God, Jesus, and the Holy Spirit really are there for you, Karen—just believe! I should divulge, in the interest of full disclosure, that this boyfriend had a shaved head and an amazing smile, which was *really* the attraction, and I went along for the ride to church.

It was around this time that some of my drill team girlfriends were in a horrible car crash. It was early morning on a typical foggy, fall Texas day as they were heading to school and they landed in a barrow pit with the little VW Bug smashed around them. Our friend, Kathy, was in a coma and critical condition for months. I believe the prayers we all said for her helped in her recovery because she was able to graduate with us on time after losing almost a year to recovery and rehabilitation. I remember the conversations with Mama about "Why?" What really still resonates is that once she was getting better and I had my answer that God was looking out for us ... I just lapsed into autopilot and went on with my daily life, not continuing the journey of faith I was being shown. It seems so surreal now.

Mark and I with one of mom's stylish creations at the Prom in 1975.

As the teen years were in full swing, there was another fork in the road that proved too big to navigate with the emotional skill set I had at the time. I'd been dating Mark for only six months when out of the blue he broke up with me. *LOVE of MY LIFE*. Major heartbreak ... major loss of trust in men and myself ... need I say more girls? He was going to college and I was a senior. I think he got scared, but that could be ego talking too! We danced around being together, then apart, together, and then apart for the next year until I was a freshman at Baylor University.

Anyway, another fork in the road came one night when he drove up to visit me at Baylor and, in a roundabout way, to see if we could make it work ... or was it to tell me about his faith and how his life had changed? In either case, I was entering my self-indulgent "me, me, me" bacchanal stage! I sure as heck wasn't gonna trust that he would take care of my heart again, even if he'd put that nickel in the drum and was saved! Funny thing was, though, I could see that Mark was more peaceful, but I didn't trust that was the way of *my* future. Trust is such a small word, but the implications on our life when it's not firmly in place are just phenomenal! I like to think God was "noodging" (an East Coast term I love to say!) me to trust him once again, but I refused to bite. Mark and I have now reconnected and shared how life turned out for us both. It's a comfort to visit and to have healed that wound and realize God was already there! One of these days—who knows—maybe there will be another ministry for me, helping young teens cope with their emotions and navigate all the heart-wrenching stumps and rocks in their path to growing up! God does close doors and open windows!

CHAPTER 3

Holy Smokes! You Want Me to Do WHAT?

I graduated from Baylor University in 1981 instead of 1980 with a B.S. in Elementary Education. I took a year off to tour with *Up With People* (*UWP*). God created a coincidence when *UWP* came and sang at Baylor my sophomore year. The freshman year had been a challenge with the ol' devil and God warring for my soul. I was feeling empty and without purpose when I saw they were coming to perform that night. I took it as a sign that maybe I should give it a try! We had a few girls with *UWP* stay at our home in Houston when I was in high school and it left quite an impression upon me. So, after the performance when they asked if anybody wanted to sign up for an interview ... yepper, I skedaddled on up and nailed the interview ... then ... how to tell Daddy it would "only cost a dollar a day."

I told him I would get a part-time job during the college year, which I did at Albertson's, checking groceries to offset some expenses, and continued to lifeguard and teach swim lessons in the summer. I think they both knew how much I wanted to go to *UWP* because even though I'd always worked babysitting, lifeguarding, clerking, etc. I just wasn't one to check groceries with codes to be entered in by hand in the register. My grades improved and I was more mindful of the cash-flow impact on a hard-working fella raising a family of four kids on one salary with a stay-at-home mom!

My Cast C teammates and I staged our show in Tucson, Arizona the summer of 1979 then hit the road, first to Canada, then across the USA and over to Europe before heading home for Christmas. You truly have to believe in the *UWP* ideals of leadership, integrity, and service to last the entire year, singing and working mostly fifteen- to eighteen-hour days. I remember the small breakout show at a cerebral palsy center in Europe like it was yesterday. Truthfully, I was always a little on edge around people with disabilities. I was unsure how to relate to them and so scared. *UWP* reinforces the humanity in all of us ALL around the world! Just because we might not speak the same language doesn't mean we can't connect through music! So, I sucked it up and smiled my way through our songs while holding hands of those who didn't understand a word we were singing but who had megawatt smiles and head shakes in time with the tunes. There was a peaceful feeling that came over me as the tears slipped out of my eyes … as if God were revealing to me the way forward. Of course, I didn't know it at the time but that the memory would remind me: God's already there. My best *UWP* friend, Ray, in 2004 nominated me for the J. Blanton Belk (*UWP* Founder) Outstanding Alumni Award and surprised me when they announced I'd won for founding the SWF … God's already there!

I finished up the amazing year with *UWP*, grateful for the lifelong friendships forged in the fire of giving. I returned to complete my Baylor degree, interview for, and get a job teaching fifth grade in my old school district, Klein ISD. It was so much fun teaching school and seeing how much the kids changed from the beginning to the end of the school year. I had a picture of a little girl posted in the coat closet which read, "God don't make no junk!" I wanted all my kids to know they were to be treasured and that my classroom was a safe place to learn (maybe stemming from my innate bashfulness?). In 1983, my high school friend, Bridget, set me up on a blind date with a fella from her workplace. Kirk Ball called and invited me to a comedy club but I told him I had to first stay for my brother's birthday celebration … family first. Luckily, he wasn't dissuaded! We had a fun time leading to many more dates and eventually a proposal.

Left: Ok MOO, if you say so! Right: Bev, Gramma Lou, Kaelin, and Me.

Kirk came from a good Iowa family that was not quite as close as our family. He has solid roots and is a loyal man and father. I remember he made me laugh and I knew deep in my bones he would stay a stand-up fella. Little did I know how cherished and important that trait would be! I also asked God to guide me and show me how to have the faith needed to leave my family after a year of marriage to move to Denver. I REALLY didn't want to leave Houston and move to Denver, but Kirk had accepted a job in the oil industry. We bought our first home, which was fun as I held down part-time administrative jobs until I became pregnant and could be a stay-at-home mom. Be careful what you wish for, eh! I had morning sickness for almost eight months and then they had to induce because that lil' person growing inside of me just didn't want to come out … gee, I wonder if she knew what was ahead?

Mama flew up from Houston for a week to ease me into motherhood and just be the best mama ever! Kaelin Ball finally arrived via C-section during a snowstorm and a Broncos football game, weighing in at nine pounds, fourteen and three-quarter ounces, and twenty-one inches. Your life, no doubt like mine, has never been the same since the delivery that brought Sturge-Weber syndrome into your life. I saw out of my sleepy eyes a whirlwind of activity by the OR staff to hustle Kaelin out of the OR as I drifted off in a fog of pharmaceuticals. I woke up in my hospital room which I shared with a young teen mom who had a "perfect baby" and natural delivery. it slowly dawned on me that something was wrong. Where were Kaelin and Kirk and Mom? A glaucoma specialist, Dr. Allan Eisenbaum, had been called in to look at her left eye, which was cloudy and enlarged. This was all unbeknownst to me, but afterward they said she'd need eye surgery in just a few days to reduce her eye pressure. We were released from the hospital amid a river of tears and fears and we went directly to Dr. Eisenbaum's office. I can still see in my mind's eye the looks of pity from those in the waiting room ... me trying to shield Kaelin and trying not to look and see the fear in my Mama's eyes too. I'd let them all down. Her delivery was not the fairytale one I'd envisioned for a lifetime. I was too mired in postpartum issues and having a whale of a pity party to truly think about what Kirk must be thinking. I just wanted to get home, away from staring eyes, and hide. There would be a new world filled with five-syllable-long eye surgery procedures, medication, and appointment schedules—and I was in no hurry to embrace it!

Her first eye surgery was at one week old, then one month old and then three months old ... and every day in between in the doctor's office ... welcome to your life lil' one! Is it the same with you, dear reader, that you can remember some of those early days like a seared scar and other days as a total blur of tiredness and fear?

I was recovering enough from the C-section and getting adjusted to our new world after Kaelin had her third glaucoma surgery while Kirk was sifting through medical bills like he was playing solitaire. My Mom had taken time off work to stay with us the first week, and what a huge blessing she was as we were both in such shock. Her deep faith and calm presence guided us through and set us up to succeed.

The days and months flew by as we waited for the inevitable seizures with hopeful but bated breath and a hitch in our throats every time Kaelin twitched. Once the third glaucoma surgery was done, the ol' Irish, German, and Scottish stubbornness kicked in at high gear! Kirk was driving us to a neurology appointment and Kaelin was nestled in my arms. I looked down at Kaelin and knew that I needed to move mountains for her. Methodists don't talk that much about the Holy Spirit in an everyday "oh yeah, he's talking to YOU" type manner. So, as I looked down at her, my calling was born. I just *knew* God had some plans, and it would be ok, and the fear subsided for a bit. It still was a moment though where I said in my heart, "You want me to do WHAT?" I took a big gulp and committed to answer that call with a lil' caveat ... if he would just please keep her "normal." I know, I know—you aren't supposed to bargain with God because it does no good, and shucks, what kind of faith does that show

First SWF Fundraiser at Aurora Methodist Church.

anyway? The old fears of raising a handicapped child like those I saw at the Cerebral Palsy center were building. I think He knew that to go out into the world and spread His news and build an international network, Kirk and I would both need that blessing for Kaelin to be cognitively "normal." Eternally grateful is an understatement!

We decided to start the Sturge-Weber Foundation in January 1987 to do more than just cry and wait ... we needed answers! Our neurologist, Dr. Richard Finkel, worked with us to spread the word and reach out to other neurologists at an annual Child Neurology Society meeting. Slowly, the phone calls and letters came in and we formed an expanding group of volunteers from Pittsburgh, Houston, Oklahoma City, and beyond. Our "normal" had changed, but Kaelin's smiling face, beautiful blue eyes, and ever-progressing milestones gave us renewed hope.

A week before Kaelin's first birthday we took a break from all the medical and financial worries and packed a diaper bag filled with Phenergan and lots of supplies to hike the trails in the Rocky Mountains for an afternoon. Glorious fall foliage and such peace ... we hadn't known the like for a year. I truly thought we'd have those seizures beat.

Later the following week, I left Kaelin with my neighbor for just a few hours—remember there were no cell phones back then. I was meeting Kaelin's dermatologist for lunch and trying to entice Dr. Joe Morelli to join our inaugural medical advisory board. When I got home, Kaelin was throwing up and my neighbor and I thought she might be getting the flu. The rest of the afternoon Kaelin was getting weaker and in my gut, I knew we had to go to the Emergency Room (ER)—but my heart was shattered. Kirk and I took her to the ER when her arm started jerking and her head wouldn't change position ... Seizures 1, Kaelin 0. After a week in the hospital, we got the seizures under control and were released in time for her first birthday party. Family, food, faith, and always laughter, even in the face of adversity! Life *is* about the celebrations! There is *always* something to celebrate and exude the joy God wants us to feel and to give to others. My mom and dad flew up to celebrate with us, my cousins, my aunt and uncle, my brother, and family friends too. Daddy—when he first held Kaelin—looked down and said something to the effect of her face had a beautiful lil' heart on it. It was such a comfort and healing moment!

Seizures may have won the first round in our fight with SWS, but they weren't going to win the game, set, match, or war I'd declared

Left: Ball family 1993. Right: Ball family 2018.

Betty Ford Award Winners: Sarah and Jim Brady and Kirk and Karen Ball. *My cherished angel Aunt Carlene with Michael M.*

on Sturge-Weber syndrome! The laser treatments didn't stop and the celebrations with food and friends didn't either! My Aunt Carlene was a Godsend during the early years. She would accompany us to laser treatments and give Kirk and me a much-needed break for "date night." She and my Uncle Bruce also helped us organize an onslaught of more than 500 pieces of mail in our kitchen and living room that we received in answer to an Ann Landers column article that Anita M. wrote to gain Sturge-Weber syndrome awareness.

The Ann Landers column and a *Denver Post* article were the first public relations awareness articles to put the SWF into the public domain. First Lady Betty Ford happened to see the *Post* article around the time of the Beaver Creek Hyatt Grand Opening. Betty reached out to honor former Press Secretary Jim Brady and his wife Sarah as National recipients, and Kirk and me as Colorado recipients.

Once we got Kaelin's seizures and glaucoma under control and the daily therapy sessions went down to zero, it was time to think about a new addition to the family and a buddy for Kaelin. Derek was born on February 24, 1993. We were so ecstatic ... no birthmark and healthy! They scheduled me to be induced, fearing another nearly ten-pound delivery, but alas, he came in just under eight pounds. Little did we know that we would have unique battles with autism and ADHD to go to war with for him! A lifetime of extra out-of-pocket expenses for speech and occupational therapy as well as out-of-district special schooling; a slew of angels that

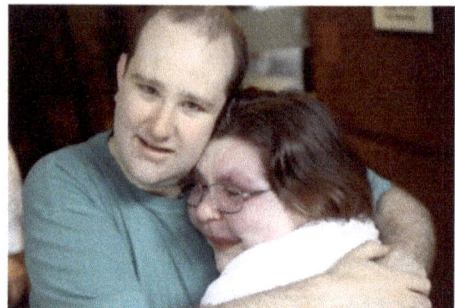

Still loving each other!

were teachers, ABA therapists, and *always* family love and support whenever it was needed to shepherd Derek through life.

Today, Derek lives in a Christian group home in Montana and is "living large" as he says as a diehard Broncos fan! His story is for another time and another book! Warrior Mama is an understatement as you might imagine for lil' ol' me!

It's important in any battle for you to name your enemy. I've found that to be true with Sturge-Weber—and really, any challenges that touch your life that are fought on various frontlines at home and in public. I nicknamed one enemy the "Numb and Dazed syndrome" in an early SWF publication. You know the one, where you get some bad news, or a seizure pops up out of the blue and your world is rocked to its core. It sets you off into a kind of numb and dazed state of shock. I will always remember the deluge of fear and panic that set in when she was having her first seizure!

You are better able to focus and create a plan for how to defeat the enemy when you name it. There are a plethora of emotions that ebb and flow in each challenge you face or each medical crisis. The first enemy that comes on with a vengeance is FEAR. The best way I've found, and many other warriors have too, is to learn all you can about the enemy that's driving that fear. No sense reinventing the wheel either! Reach out to healthcare providers, other parents, or individuals who have trod the same path you're currently facing—and by all means hit the internet (armed with the knowledge that some advice is not one-size-fits-all). Fear—like many negative emotions—is a magnet. It pulls other emotional enemies into the vortex of angst, and is toxic in too large of a dose. Defeat this enemy head-on and early to avoid physical reactions that linger and will rob the warrior of energy needed for the long haul and fight.

GUILT is oftentimes a close second enemy to fear. Again, the best way to banish this negative enemy is with knowledge and open communication. It is also recommended that the parents and immediate family support one another and seek counsel whenever needed ... sooner than later! ANXIETY and ANGER creep up all the time, even in "normal" everyday life. The same thing happens with frustration for poor communication, lack of level medications, resentment for where you are in life ... the list goes on. Deal with all these negative enemies head-on! Hug it out as often as you can, too. Take time alone as needed. Get over yourself. You will find your own routine as the years go on. Truthfully, I always wanted a room where I could throw plates and glasses or a punching bag to take out my frustrations and anger on things rather than people! I wish I had gotten that room because it would have saved words leaving my mouth I can never take back.

The family—both immediate and extended—need support from each other and the surrounding community. There are some people

BJF, my road warrior! Some nights are more memorable than others!

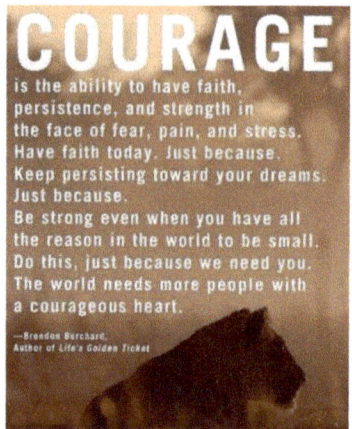

Best Family EVER!

who will never ask for help and others, that is all they do. Find a good balance, because ultimately it is our responsibility to care for our loved one with SWS or any other rare disease. We will learn what is best for them educationally, medically, socially, etc. Trust your gut instincts. Get out in nature and feel the wonder and peace it provides. Celebrate the little successes and seek joy. My immediate family, as you've read, has always found a way to laugh in the face of adversity! Some may think we're a bit strange, but it's worked for us all these years and if you haven't tried it, don't knock it!

If you're *really* lucky in life you get to also travel the road and be on the frontlines with your brother! Brian James Fisher is truly special and a "piece of work" as Daddy likes to say. He had a stellar career in the pharmaceutical industry for many years and would volunteer his time to attend industry conferences and exhibits with me. I kept telling him I really knew he was going to leave the industry and work for the SWF because God had other plans for him. He didn't scoff at it, but wasn't really ready to answer the call when I kept "noodging."

Thankfully, he did come work with us and within the first six months that he was on board he landed a $250,000 government grant which I did NOT have the expertise to tackle. *Bam!* We have been off to the races ever since and the research has sky-rocketed—and the professional level of branding has too. He has been a blessing from the moment Mama brought him home so I could play sister and pretend mama! The best is yet to be!

PART II
WARRIOR MAMAS

CHAPTER 4

Inspirational Warrior Mama Stories

I asked some of my fellow Warrior Mamas to submit their stories because, after all, this book is really about the Warrior Mama in all of us! Here are a few that took the time to "tell their tale," and will hopefully inspire and lighten your load as much as they have mine! To a woman, Warrior Mamas from around the world tell me stories of their courage, fear, guilt, and so much more.

It is always heartbreaking when you hear stories of mamas who stay rooted in self-destructive behaviors, for whatever reason. The load is too much to bear; they can't handle the self-imposed guilt, or the financial strains overwhelm them. These mamas and the tough times of their lives require the rest of us to keep reaching out, encouraging new paths of self-care, and providing credible resources to take advantage of so we can be there for our children for a lifetime.

> *"But the bravest are surely those who have the clearest vision of what is before them, glory and danger alike, and yet notwithstanding go out to meet it."*

Sara's Warrior Mama

Where do I begin? Sara is thirty-two, has SWS, and is profoundly disabled. Her birthmark is bilateral, her lips are big, her tongue sticks out most of the time, she is blind, and her brain hasn't grown since she was six months old. Her seizures are under control and she has had hundreds of eye surgeries. Sara starting have seizures at three months old and several times we were told she wasn't going to pull through. We were told Sara wouldn't live to be seven years, then she had a stroke when she was ten years old and wasn't supposed to make it. These are just a few things that make me a "Warrior Mama."

I have fought to get the education that Sara deserves. I have been to mediation on more than one occasion against school districts, and I have closed facilities that were doing illegal things. I have gotten people fired and even put in jail for hurting her and not taking responsibility for their actions.

Sara may not talk, or walk, or see; she must be fed and bathed; but she has the biggest heart of anyone I have ever met and a smile that will light up the room.

I would like to say she that got her strength from me, but I feel I got my strength from *her*. I had no idea what our family's lives would be like, but I always knew Sara would be part of it. We didn't really go places for holidays and vacations because we felt it was more important to spend the time as a family because we never knew when the last one might be.

I would tell my younger self not to be so sad, angry, and depressed, or to cry so much.

I would tell myself to laugh, to not sweat the small stuff, and instead of spending time being sad and crying, to give more hugs and love to both of my girls.

I would not have gotten angry at people that would look at Sara and laugh or point. I would have spent that time educating them, showing them that she has feelings and needs touch and love—just like them.

— *Thea B., Arizona*

Summer's Warrior Mama

Our sweet Summer was diagnosed with SWS at three weeks old due to her glaucoma and port-wine birthmark. She had her first glaucoma surgery at five weeks old, and her first seizure at three and a half months old. Her glaucoma surgeries have been very successful and thankfully, for now, her seizures are under control with Keppra and Trileptal.

My advice to mamas out there would be to be present in life. We deal with some hard stuff. It's one thing to process through issues with your own health, but when it comes to our babies it's a completely different arena. You must live in a very vulnerable place knowing you have limited resources to help your child, which we mamas have a hard time with since we want to make everything better for our little ones. Sometimes you just need a good cry—it's okay to be vulnerable sometimes. It's also very important to remember you can't stay in that 'place' for long. We must pick up and move to the other side, which births strength, love, progress, and positivity.

That has been my biggest lesson, and one I took for granted with our older children. It's okay to be sad, heartbroken, mad, scared, and whatever else you experience, but don't let it consume you. We can only control what we can control. Some things we must give to faith, and trust that there is a higher plan in the works. I pray A LOT, and I research A LOT. I know I can't take SWS away for Summer, but I can be

her best advocate and that is the only thing I have control over that I can do to help her, aside from my unconditional love and support.

Learn as much as you can, be positive in your thinking, have meltdowns ... it's ok ... even moms without special-needs children have them, so you have *certainly* earned it! But question everything—be on the continual journey of learning so you can find the best care and treatment for your child, and never lose hope. We have been told our Summer has extensive brain calcifications from her port-wine birthmark, and that due to her brain involvement, she may encounter issues with learning to sit, walk, and talk. Well—I can tell you now, we never accepted that and just a few days ago she stood all on her own, for a few seconds—at just over a year old. This may seem normal to some, but this is an amazing success for her!

Celebrate the wins, be present in the tough times, and build upon that to appreciate the good times even more. We were chosen to be these children's mamas. Enjoy this beauty you have been chosen to see. I call it my "goggles of a different view." Things are a bit brighter and feats are a bit more special, and precious moments are treasured even more. Because I have seen some of the bad, I can truly be blessed by the good. Many go through life without such a gift!

— *Beth A., B.S.*

Luka's Warrior Mama

In our country, SWS is little known, with obsolete methods of treatment. Since my son was diagnosed SWS, I struggled and struggled to learn more about the syndrome. In order to help him, I first needed to find out and get to know SWS. I found out a little from our doctors, and most of the information and help I got from SWF and Julia Terrell. This way, I would publicly thank you.

I accepted SWS with my son and at the same time I started to learn about it. For sadness and depression, I have no time; only fighting is important for us. I have made more than thirty contacts from various parts of the world, from professionals, and made a diary about it, about every test, about every change with my son. I'm always persistent. I'll never give up, while I'm alive, I'm looking for a solution. And to the end of the world if necessary, if anyone gives me some hope for his recovery.

I've never wondered, "Why is my child...?" because I will not get an answer. It's my child; I love him. If I could again, I would give birth to the same baby 100 times. I teach for him; the warrior was for him, and gave life for him. I teach him to be happy because his smile is my won battle. Many nights without sleep—as well as many days under stress—but worth it is his gaze, smile, and his words "Mama."

I was ignored many times, was thrown out when I asked for help for him, but I did not give up—I got up *every time*. Nothing will stop me, because there are people who will help me, because life is a fight in which we will win, because we will live!

At the age of three, due to a large number of daily epileptic seizures, Luka had epilepsy surgery, partial resection, and then seventy-five percent of his brain tissue was removed. After that, he was in great danger due to repeated epileptic attacks. We went through a very difficult period during and after the operation. It took us a long time to get back to normal life. With a lot of exercise, activity, and dedication, we managed to come back and continue a normal life. It is now controlled. What is extremely important in such situations is that we should always remain positive and smiling, with hope and faith in our children. What kept me strong was Luke's smile, his courage, and his life: it motivates and encourages me and gives me strength like a storm. There are no tears for us, there is no obstacle that can prevent us from achieving the goal, and that goal is to work with all our energy to improve the quality of life of our children. They are our heroes and they are the movers of our world.

— *Mila M., Serbia*

Warrior Mama's Note to Younger Self

You are a new mom with all the run-of-the-mill questions that go with being inexperienced in the most significant job in the world. Added to that you have been entrusted with a daughter with Sturge-Weber syndrome. In a fog, with no help from the internet (it hadn't been invented yet), you and your husband will navigate doctor appointments, learn what "is" and what "might be," make a necessary life changes, walk through surgeries, etc.

The love, support and prayers of family and countless friends bolster your strength and before you know it, your baby is a happy little girl enjoying life as she knows it. After a few years you are made aware of the Sturge-Weber support group (not yet a foundation) and attend a meeting or two with your daughter. You think, "I'm not really sure I need this. After all, we all seem to be doing just fine, the trabeculoplasty was successful and medication is working. We are not experiencing the varied and serious neurological and physical complications others are, we have our own support system and mainly: she doesn't want to go."

Just GO. Go to come alongside others and be an encouragement. Go to learn. Go to be equipped for what might be. Go to receive the support you (and she) don't realize you need. Yes, now you have the internet and can receive support online, but there is nothing like the personal connection that comes from being in the presence of people who KNOW.

Your story is unique in many ways. I hope you will rest in knowing there is always HOPE.

— Wishes to Remain Anonymous

Silas' Warrior Mama

Our world was rocked when our son Silas had his first seizure at nine months and was soon after diagnosed with the rare condition of Sturge Weber syndrome. Though my husband Kris and I were overwhelmed with the unknown, we were certain about one thing: we weren't going to sit idly by and be the victims of circumstance. We were going to fight!

I threw myself headfirst into every possible avenue that offered the promise of support and answers for the questions we were desperately looking for.

I immediately partnered with the Sturge-Weber Foundation—attending conferences and education days, fundraising, and embracing with pride the chance to become advocates for Sturge-Weber syndrome and the Sturge-Weber Foundation. I felt infused with purpose and started to expand my energy in all directions.

I volunteered to join the Foundation's new *Patient Engagement Network*, focused on patient-centered research. I soon found myself as the Chairperson of the P.E.N., a position two years earlier I would have never dreamed I was qualified for. I found a strength I didn't know I had as I helped lead a committee of doctors, researchers, parents, and patients coming together for the first time.

At home, I have partnered with Silas' doctors, teachers, coaches, and our community to make sure they are aware of his condition and have a plan in place should medical attention become necessary.

It never seemed to be enough. I was relentless in my pursuit of opportunities to meet this challenge head on.

The first few years made one point crystal clear: funding the research that is critical for advancing treatments and a potential cure was what was needed most. I'd spent a career in media sales and so fundraising for this cause became my mission.

In 2014, I organized our first local fundraiser event, *Rock for a Cure*, which has since been featured in our local paper, and has become a favorite annual event for our family and friends to attend. This family karaoke event is held in the fall each year, to celebrate our son's love of music and to raise awareness of Sturge Weber syndrome and epilepsy.

I extended the *Rock for a Cure* mission to social media. I created Instagram and Facebook pages to engage our growing community of supporters year-round with updates and stories on our journey as well as to highlight other families and news in the community.

This visibility helped us connect with other families and led us to participate in even more fundraising events, the most memorable being part of a team of runners for Team SWF in the iconic Falmouth Road Race on Cape Cod.

As someone who is not typically a runner, this was my most challenging fundraising and awareness event to date. Seven and a half miles of rolling hills in the height of August summer heat was a daunting challenge. But I had all the motivation I needed to help me cross that finish line.

Through all our awareness and fundraising events, we have raised nearly $50,000 for the Sturge Weber Foundation during the past seven years—a number I would have never dreamed possible.

A number that I also know is a small fraction of what is needed. So, the fight continues!

I am lucky to have met and partnered with many other Warrior Moms who join this fight and help to raise more than I can do alone.

I've always had a bit of a mama bear spirit, long before I had children, so having a child with a rare disease has only heightened that instinct. The path is not always clear, and there have been moments when we may have gone in the wrong direction, but the one thing that is crystal clear is that my son will not travel this journey alone.

I will fight, alongside all of my Warrior Mama friends, to ensure that he and his Sturge-Weber friends are given every opportunity available to them.

— *Kellie S., Illinois*

Stephen's Warrior Mama

There are very many things to consider when trying to decide what is best for the family as well as for the person with SWS. Stephen is now sixty-two, but back then, services for children with disabilities were few and difficult to come by. Back then, children with disabilities were determined to be either educable or trainable. If they were educable, you might try to fight your way to get him into a classroom and have him live at home. If he were only trainable, good luck. By the time Stephen was eight, we had four older children and were expecting another. With few choices, our family was advised to "institutionalize" him. It was heartbreaking but God is good, and we made it work.

We visited him often in Staten Island, New York, at the Willowbrook State School. As we did not have a car then, we used public transportation, taking two hours to use a train, subway, ferry, and local bus. We took one of the other children with us each time and they thought it was an adventure. We took Stephen home for a summer vacation and on holidays because we always wanted to make sure he grew up knowing his brothers and sisters.

I cannot count the number of times I looked back with tears in our eyes and saw him watching us leave those grounds. We had approached the public school when he was five, but there was no law then that they had to take him. The ARC had a small program in our county, but the family had to transport him, and we did not have a car then. Local agencies turned us down for lack of facilities or programs. I was therefore in a position to testify in federal court with other parents about the disaster that was Willowbrook. We advocated at all levels for services in the community because the state school did not have adequate educational services and the children were in wards of eighty or more.

In 1975, we were successful in a lawsuit against the State of New York in having the school closed and in creating group homes. We had worked with the Civil Liberties Union and many public interest lawyers and with a young TV journalist. Now, with the internet, you can learn all about our struggles by searching Willowbrook State School (such a sweet name for a horrid place).

Now Stephen lives in a home near us with twenty-four-hour staffing and goes to an OT program. He has lived there forty years with seven other people, happily. He is settled in a good home, in the community near us, is given good medical care, has friends, and is valued.

He cannot read except for simple advertising signs and he marks the calendar for visiting days. He cannot dial the phone but loves to answer it and chat when we call.

It is my firm belief that Stephen came into this world for a reason—a reason that did not appear to be within our expectations or planning. But God is the Divine Planner and author of all good, so our family is grateful that Stephen is here.

— *Ann N., New York*

Céline's Warrior Mama

Céline Gerry Brewbaker was born August 10, 2016, at 7:23 p.m. in my bathroom, and she literally fell into my life. I began having contractions at 3:30 a.m. that day. We went to the hospital at 9:00 a.m. to get checked, and I was only dilated at one centimeter so they sent me home and told me to come back when the contractions were consistently five minutes apart and felt different. I went home and worked all day from a laptop, and about 5:00 p.m. my contractions got worse, but not consistent. I had my husband, Kevin, drive me to a prenatal yoga class, which I thought would help distract me from the pain. The contractions got worse halfway through class, but of course, I had him drive me home, so we could feed our two-year-old son, before heading to the hospital. Within fifteen minutes of being home, my water broke on the toilet, and I frantically told my husband to call 911, while our two-year-old was strapped in his high-chair screaming. My husband ran back and forth between the bathroom, where I was, and the kitchen, where our son was. The 911 operator told me to get off the toilet and lay down on the floor. Before I could lay down, as I was standing up, I had one more big contraction and out the baby came onto the floor. My poor husband had to tie off the umbilical cord and try and comfort our son, while getting a towel to wrap the baby in. The ambulance arrived about five minutes later, checked us both out, and they took me and the baby to the hospital.

At the hospital, they checked Baby Céline over, and told me she would need to go to NICU for the night because she had hit her head during her birth and they wanted to do several tests and keep her under observation for the night. It was traumatic for me, realizing how she was born, and it was very hard being separated from my baby, but I went and saw her every two hours to nurse her. She was the biggest, healthiest baby in the NICU. The next morning another doctor looked at her and determined she needed further testing which involved an eye test (where they pried her eyes open with a forceful tool), ultrasound of the liver, and an MRI of the brain. They told us that evening that if the tests were normal, she could be brought to stay in my room with me. At midnight, they told us the tests were normal and they brought her to me. The next afternoon, a pediatrician from our son's doctor's office came to the hospital to check her over, and she delivered us heartbreaking news. It turned out that the radiologist who read the MRI results in the evening, did so incorrectly. A pediatric radiologist re-read the test in the morning and we were told that Céline has abnormal blood capillaries around her brain, which is associated with a condition called Sturge-Weber syndrome. I was in shock and all I could think of was how this might affect my son. How much will his life be inconvenienced by a special needs sister? Will he get enough attention? How much wouldn't she be able to do?

The first month with her at home was really hard. We didn't know what infant seizures looked like, and I felt responsible for her being born with such a heartbreaking diagnosis. Was it something I did during pregnancy? Was it because her father was much older than the average father? Kevin found the Sturge Weber Foundation right when we got home from the hospital and learned (at that time before they identified the gene mutation) that the cause of SWS was totally random and not our fault.

Fast forward thirteen months later: On September 5, 2017, Celine began having her first focal seizures, where her right hand would shake, her eyes would dart to the right, and her left calf and foot would shake. She was crying uncontrollably for about an hour prior to when the seizures began. Kevin picked her out of her crib when the shaking stopped and tried to get her to sit up and she was unable to. We rushed her to C.S. Mott's Children's Hospital as fast as we could, because she was conscious and breathing fine. She spent twelve days in the hospital. Her seizures were nonexistent for several months, with a few instances of seizures here and there, then they returned with vengeance in March 2019, leading to a longer hospital stay and more medications. We spent that summer having Celine evaluated for a full hemispherectomy and spoke with doctors in Michigan, New York, Maryland, and Boston, who all recommended she have the surgery as soon as we were ready. We decided that we were most comfortable with C.S. Mott's Children's Hospital's neurosurgeon, who was very familiar with the added risks of brain surgery on a Sturge-Weber child.

On September 20, 2020, Celine endured a ten-hour surgery to disconnect the left side of her brain from the right. She awoke from the surgery able to speak and even ate pancakes with a fork by herself the next day. She stayed in the hospital for a month for in-patient rehab, and she did lose the use of her right hand (it is a helper hand at times) and has a hitch in her right step. Her visual field cut also got worse on the right. She trips and runs into walls easily, but she always gets back up again. She's got a huge team of doctors and therapists in multiple specialties; managing all of them has taught me to be assertive, organized, and adamant. She was recently diagnosed with ADHD, but is thriving in preschool with the help of an aide.

Managing appointments and surgeries (or lack of) during COVID-19 has taught me to never settle for less than how my daughter should ethically be treated, and that it's ok to question even the best hospital. For instance, when they want to test your asymptomatic three-year-old twice in one week (because she has two OR procedures) for a virus that rarely affects children, and when you refuse that test, they tell you they're going to give her an IV while she's awake because you refused to traumatize her with another unnecessary test.

Being a mom to a four-year-old with complex medical needs, it's challenging to know what to say when she looks at me and says, "I don't want to go to the "ospital." Celine has had twenty-eight pulsed-dye laser treatments on the Port Wine Stain birthmarks that take up almost half of her body, four glaucoma eye surgeries, two muscle eye surgeries, a skin biopsy, Botox to help with hemiparesis on her right hand, at least eight EEGS, five MRIs, two CT scans, two PET scans, and physical and occupational therapy two to three times a week for most of her life. Celine is now asking about her birthmarks, AFO, surgeries, etc., and expressing that she's had enough anesthesia. It brings about tough choices for parents because all of her care is medically necessary, but it comes to a point where her mental health needs to be prioritized—and enough is enough; she needs a break.

If I could give my younger, "new" special-needs mom-self some advice, I'd tell her to take this one day, one hour, one minute at a time. It's important to appreciate a baby for being a baby and enjoy the moment. I've also learned that self-care and putting one's marriage as a priority is vital to survive this. I make time to ride horses, talk to a therapist, read, and practice yoga, and my family has always been supportive to make sure we each get a break. Communication and time as a couple without kids is essential! In the words of Celine's namesake, Celine Dion (who we met when Baby Celine was nine months old), "There are two days you can do nothing about: yesterday and tomorrow. Today is a great day."

Raising a child with Sturge-Weber syndrome is a war, and each battle has made me stronger.

— Deborah B., Michigan

Marissa's Warrior Mama

My Mom taught me two things from a young age that have guided me through life. The first was that if you don't have something nice to say, then you say nothing at all. The second was to always follow your gut feeling. As a Mom, now I understand why these were the two principles to live by. I added one more from my experience and that was to never accept the answer "no," because the next question should always be "OK, then how can I get this done?" I believe these three guiding principles are what makes you a Warrior! The Mama for me came on March 24, 2009, when Marissa was born.

After many years of trying, in 2008 we were pregnant with our daughter Marissa. We were so lucky—it was our tenth year of marriage when she would arrive, and the best present ever. The pregnancy was perfect, and after twenty hours of labor Marissa arrived. She was beautiful. I was in love—and then I heard things like, "Will that go away?" "That is pretty dark." "What can we do?" I didn't know how to respond, except to ask to see her again. I took one look and I saw the purple birthmark and her eye swollen shut and thought, "Well, she can't go to school like that, can she?"

The next morning, we were visited by so many people who had the same negative expression and were told that she might have Sturge ... what? She may have glaucoma. Old people have glaucoma, right? How? I always say that it was the revolving door of craziness.

Fast forward some and Marissa was doing well: growing, laughing, and hitting milestones. At four months old, I felt that she was being treated like a piece of a puzzle by each doctor, and that no one treated her like a whole puzzle. I reached out to Anne Howard at the Sturge Weber Foundation, and before we knew it I was on my way to northern New Jersey to meet our new family that would become "our people." We were in the lobby and this woman who is larger than life came right up to me and snatched up Marissa and hugged her tight and loved her. Didn't stare at her birthmark, didn't ask any questions; she just told me how adorable she was! Ahhh ... I finally felt normalcy of some kind, and that was the day we came home. Little did we know that the larger than life Mamma we met was our very own Karen Ball.

You see, what I learned that weekend was tremendous. I learned it is ok to be different. I now can say "Yes, I am ready for the fight of my life," as one mom asked me. I learned to stop and take a break when I get overwhelmed. I always allow myself forty-eight hours to dwell on any news, put it in the back of my brain, and let Marissa write her story.

After this pivotal weekend, I found I had the passion and determination (I always had) and that, coupled with this new fire, I would not fail Marissa. Over the years I have been able to fight for her education—not just in IEP meetings, but in court when they denied her rights. I have learned and researched so much for her needs in education and keep finding new ways to do things. I have been successful in advocating for her with doctors, specialists, and many more. I have advocated for her and with her on Capitol Hill. We have joined our congressman at a roundtable to inform the public about prescription drugs and rare diseases. The best part? We don't take no for an answer; we always ask, "If not, then what can we do?"

Marissa at the young age of eleven is so powerful. I hope she always sees herself through my eyes as I try to look at myself through her eyes with the same amount of adoration. The funny part is it took a little baby with a rare disease to discover my inner Warrior Mama! I always say, who knows how this will go and what will happen at any given time, but I am not afraid anymore. I know that no matter what her smile alone has always told me everything will work out!! At the moment of any one of her smiles, I remember to *Just Breathe!*

—*Julia T., New Jersey*

Danny's Warrior Mama

On June 28, 1983, my life changed forever. That was the day my son, Daniel Mark Keffer was born. I knew something was wrong when the room quickly fell completely silent and the nurses wouldn't let me see what was going on. Danny was born with a port wine stain on the left side of his face that wrapped around the back of his head, and the medical staff initially thought it was because he wasn't getting enough oxygen. That was when our journey began.

The emotional roller coaster started when I was initially told that it was a birthmark that would disappear as he got older, and to not worry, and that he was perfectly healthy and would lead a normal life. At first, I was amazed that not only did he meet his developmental goals, he met them earlier than a "typical" infant. I stopped worrying about his development. Then when he was almost seven months old he began to have seizures. At first, even as a nurse, I didn't know they were seizures because they were infantile spasms, just a quick jerking of his head. When they became more pronounced, I took him to the pediatrician and from an x-ray of his skull he was diagnosed with Sturge-Weber syndrome. Nobody—not even the "experts" at Children's Hospital of Pittsburgh—could give me any information on SWS, and I was told that

due to the severity of the disease, he would not make it to his first birthday. The psychology "expert" told me to institutionalize him because it wouldn't be fair to my other children.

Fast forward four years to 1987. I saw a tiny advertisement in the "Exceptional Parent's Magazine" that described SWS and had a phone number to call. It took four years to finally talk to a mother in Colorado who had just had a daughter born with SWS: Introduce Karen Ball. She was just the person I needed to finally feel like I could move forward and actually do something to help my son instead of just worrying and watching him fall further behind in his development. I like to think of us as the Dynamic Duo. I was Robin to her Batman. She made me do things I never would have considered doing, like fundraising and advocating in a world without computers and internet.

I come from a large family (three sisters and three brothers), but we lived in an economically depressed area. The steel mills were closing down and everyone was out of a job, but every year we would have a SWS Benefit that included two family bands (one boys and one girls), selling food and drinks, and having a Chinese Auction. Karen used to laugh because my family donated the food and the beer and provided the entertainment, and then we would buy back the things we donated. She would always say "How do you do that"? It became a much-anticipated community event with everyone emptying out their pockets to make sure we beat the previous year's record. Over the years we raised more than $200,000. To this day Karen will tell you that, in the early days especially, those benefits kept the SWF alive and kicking. *(Karen's Two Cents: That IS the truth! Between Melanie Wood and the Keffer Clan, we morphed ahead in advocacy and patient engagement. I attended the events to support all their hard work, but as the Clan knows it was also so I could compete in Workers of Job-Ziggy Ziggy Zag.)*

I finally felt that I was doing something positive that would maybe not so much help my son but would help all the families struggling with a diagnosis of SWS to have a support system. As the years went on, I had to be Danny's voice. I always say he is my soul and I am his physical body. His development stopped at six months old, so he never walked or talked, he had daily seizures, and he was almost completely blind. I still had my bad days when I would cry because my son would never play baseball and I would never get to hear him say "I love you mom." When I was down, Karen would push me back up (not pick me up) and say, "OK now, what should we do?" I did the same for her, I hope.

I had to fight for everything! The proper medical treatments, therapies, and the insurance companies. My biggest battle was his right to a free and appropriate education. The School Psychologist actually said, "My dog has a higher IQ than your son" when I wanted to get Danny in a school that would address all of his needs. Then I had to fight again when I decided he really needed to be in the high school of the district I lived and worked in so he could interact with "regular" aged peers.

Danny had three wonderful and supportive sisters. When I wanted to bring him to our high school, I checked with his sister Lindsay first because they were only two years apart and would graduate the same year. Trying to always balance attention was a constant struggle. Lindsay was cheer captain and very popular so I worried it might affect her in a negative way. Not only did she embrace the idea, Danny was immediately swept into the spotlight by the whole cheer squad, football players, and then the entire school. He even went to the prom. Lindsay used to laugh and say now I am just called Danny Keffer's sister. I can look back and say it's not what the school did for him but what he did for the school by making students more accepting of differences. For a boy that couldn't talk he certainly touched numerous lives and hearts forever.

Of course, as the years went by his health deteriorated. I was no longer worrying that today might be the day he may not wake up, but I always felt like it was a race against time. I was constantly making decisions based on his quality of life versus quantity. SWS was still a work in progress, and as he grew older we went to The Johns Hopkins Hospital. By that time his endocrine system was being affected. They may no longer say that SWS is progressive, but for Danny it certainly was. It affected deeper tissues of his brain and he needed numerous treatments and medications to maintain his level of functioning. He was the subject of many studies and provided tissue and blood samples that eventually led to the discovery of the DNA misstep that causes SWS. In many ways Danny blazed the trail of SWS research. That's what I try to remember when I look back.

Eventually SWS did cause his death. I would say it was still the ignorance and non-educated medical community that caused his death, and I wonder every day if I did enough. Maybe if I tried harder he would still be here. His immune system was compromised and he was diagnosed incorrectly and put on the wrong antibiotics by the local community hospital. As I watched him struggle to breathe and seeing his oxygen level decrease even while on oxygen, I reverted back to what I always had to do: trust my instincts. I put him in the back of the van with his portable O2 and drove two hours to a bigger hospital where he was intubated and put on a ventilator within thirty minutes. He was stabilized and in ICU.

One thing you learn as a parent of a SWS child is that you never leave their side, especially in a hospital. I was reluctantly talked into putting a tracheotomy in because he had to be on a ventilator for a month.

The ENT inserted the wrong size trach, blaming it on Danny's "unusual" body type (short and fat), and Danny went into cardiac arrest. Of all the times I thought he might not pull through, nothing prepared me to be standing outside his room, alone, and hearing the medical staff say, "We don't have a pulse; start CPR," not once, or twice, but three times he had to be resuscitated, until they figured out that they had the wrong size trach. The worst part was the attitude of the doctor telling me I was "lucky" they did anything at all because he really had no quality of life. I was stunned yet again at how cruel and ignorant many professionals still were. He went for eighteen minutes without oxygen and I was told he would lose the little bit of brain function he had left and I was asked did I really want to keep him on life support. The only thing I wanted at that time was to keep him alive long enough to allow his sisters to say goodbye, and they had to travel overnight to get there. I was prepared after that incident but Danny had his own will and he slowly got better. I insisted then that I take him home and care for him and had to go against medical advice (AMA).

Danny came home after six weeks in ICU. I brought him home on a ventilator, a feeding tube, and IV medications; at the time he was non-responsive. After a month of me caring for him, he got off of the ventilator and, except for still needing oxygen, was back to his usual self. The doctors were amazed of course, and I was looking forward to having his trach removed so he could go back to swimming. Just as my hopes were high and we had the appointment set, he had a difficult night. He was restless and seemed to be having an unusual number of seizures. He finally seemed to be resting comfortably around 4:00 a.m. and I crawled into bed beside him. An hour later his pulse ox alarm went off, and Danny had decided to leave this world just as he came in: in my arms, in his own bed, in his own way. He passed at 5:15 a.m. on 5/15/15. I am still trying to figure out if that means anything. When he passed, he took a big part of me with him because he was my other half, my soul and my purpose in life. He would have been thirty-two in June. So much for the experts.

Now, five years later, I find myself with many of the same questions I had in the beginning. Why, Why, Why! Why Danny? Why was he more affected than most of the other SWS population? Why didn't I do more? Why didn't the medical community do more? Why did he have to die then, when he had just fought his way back against all odds and he was going to be fine? Why hasn't this emotional roller coaster stopped? I am back to the beginning, alone, and still wondering if I did enough. Then I have to remind myself that if Karen and I never stopped asking why we would never have gotten this far on our journey.

So, don't stop asking why. Don't accept that you can't make a difference. And most of all don't get complacent and think that everything will be fine because it may be just that moment that changes your life forever. We all must be Warrior Moms and keep asking "Why" until we have all of our questions answered. I pray that will happen in my time because I have devoted my life to it. I haven't given up Danny's cause just because he isn't physically here.

To Karen and her wonderful, supportive family who have always been there for me when I needed it, I dedicate this lovingly to you!

— *Kathy K., Delaware*

Myla's Warrior Mama

As a young couple, just married ten months before, we were first-time parents and had no idea what to expect. Simply excited to be expecting our first child. We knew we were going to be having a little girl. When she arrived we heard the words "Oh, don't worry, that's just a mark that will fade with time. It'll be gone by the time she is one!" Again, we were first-time parents and had no reason to question that statement.

Time passed and we loved life and our little girl grew and we thought things were going great! But by the time she was seven months old things took quite a bit of a turn. One night we were playing in our living room with our spunky, happy little girl and went to put her to bed and then she woke up screaming and crying and we could not console her, which was very unlike her. I went to pick her up and rock her and the next moment I knew I was falling asleep in the chair.

A little bit later I woke and looked down and knew that something was not right. Myla was not responding to me and her eyes were looking one way and her left side was shaking. That was the night she had her first seizure. The night I became a "Warrior Mama," the night we came to know that our little girl had Sturge Weber syndrome (SWS).

If there is one thing I could tell myself as a mom of a child with SWS it's that I am not alone. We are not alone. As much as it feels that way in the moment, and that week when she was going through those first horrible seizures, remember that you are not alone. Many people out here have been through this. Yes, Sturge-Weber syndrome is different in everyone but all of us know how it feels to get the news that your child has "Sturge-Weber syndrome," your child has glaucoma, your child has a brain malformation. You just have to know that you can reach out to any of us.

When Myla was diagnosed I felt lost and didn't know who to talk to or reach out to. When I found the Sturge-Weber Foundation I discovered those people were like me in a sense. I felt like I belonged to a family. It made me feel so much better to know I could talk to people that may feel the same way as I do or have had the same experiences as me and my family.

What I've learned about myself is that I really am stronger than I thought. Going through hundreds of seizures with a seven-month-old really pulls at your strength, and putting your daughter through many treatments and doctors' appointments is not easy. You have to be strong and stand up to people when you do not believe that is what is best for your child. You come to realize that you really are stronger than you thought you were.

As a mother I am stronger now than I thought I ever was. What I am most proud of about Myla is that in her short five years of life she is the strongest, most determined little girl I have ever met. She is very weak on her left side and was very late to speak. She is now talking very well and it took her a long while to walk. She is walking very well now but still stumbles a little bit. Anything that she needs help doing she will try her hardest at doing before she asks for help. She is very determined and works so hard—she would not be where she is today if it was not for her hard work and determination.

I am so proud of her determination to work through her struggles. Myla fights through everything. When she was having seizures she would fight through no matter what; she would not want to sit, she would want to get up and play. Her determination is so admirable.

My hope for Myla's future is that she keeps up her fighting attitude no matter what her future holds. I hope she stays seizure-free and that her health stays the way it is right now, but no matter what I hope that her determination remains strong. Her attitude about everything is amazing. I hope she realizes that she can do anything she puts her mind to, no matter her situation. She has such a beautiful heart and I hope she keeps her love for the world.

To any future moms out there: Yes, the Sturge-Weber syndrome world is terrifying. It's such a rare world to be in or to join. Trust me, when we first joined we did not know what to do or think. Here are my suggestions. Number one: PLEASE do not Google. Googling is a terrible thing to do! I advise you to join the Sturge-Weber Foundation. It is full of amazing people who are willing to help at the drop of a hat! The Foundation has amazing information! Also, don't stare at your child, waiting for them to have that next seizure—that will only make you crazy. Enjoy your child. That is what they need, a sane and loving mama—as hard as that may be! Take it day-by-day, and when issues arise deal with them right away; don't wait for them to grow. Enjoy your child on the good days :)

— Thomas and Molly Speer

Millie's Warrior Mama

Author's note: This is a past reflection that many of the Warrior Mamas can relate to in some way.

Well ... I have kind of avoided this moment all day. I think because it brings back some very real and raw emotions that I don't wish on anyone. It is Millie's first birthday and yes, we are celebrating her and the year that she has had—but I am also remembering the best and worst day of a mother's life: the birth of your child and the moment you realize something is wrong. You want to so badly to be excited and celebrate life but really, you are worried out of your mind and terrified of the future. But now that it has been a year I would like to share some things I have learned over the past twelve months.

I am titling this "A year ... a letter to my daughter"

There are many things that I have learned over this past year; many about myself and many about others.

1. I learned that I am just one person ... and it takes a village. I really mean it. My support system is what has kept me sane through this whole process. I could not have been half the mom that I have been for Millie if it weren't for the people in my life. My mom has been a saving grace in picking up the slack from where I have failed. My husband has let me cry, be a total bitch, cry, and lose it—all while not judging me and giving me grace when I do not deserve it. My children have dealt with the "I forgot," the "I can't be there" and the "I'm sorry" with

such maturity and compassion that it's brought me to tears several nights. My sister and brother-in-law have given me encouragements and compliments that have stuck with me throughout the year. My brother has fed me when I would not eat. My friends have listened and given advice when I needed it the most. My community has mowed my lawn, made dinner for my family when I could not, took my kids to the pool or to ball games when we were busy with Millie, and prayed so hard I could feel it radiating off of them. And my work family ... what can I say? I am truly the luckiest person to work for them and be able to say with pride that I am part of their team. Hopefully, I have said thank you to all of them and if I have not I promise you have made a huge impact on me and my family and you deserve a straight shot to heaven in my book. Thank you from the bottom of my heart.

2. I have learned to have patience.... I always thought I was a very patient person, and maybe I am, but I have learned that when your child is "fancy," you need even more patience. You need patience with the milestones that she might or might not make. You need patience with the doctors that take FOREVER to make decisions or appointments. Your need patience in not hurrying up the future just because you are nosey and want to know what Millie will be like in 20 years. You just need patience....

3. I have learned to forgive ... forgive myself and others. I have learned to forgive myself for forgetting to order more meds on a Friday at 4:30 when the pharmacy closes at 5:00 because I have 20 other meds to worry about refilling every month. I have learned to forgive myself that if I forget she has a therapy at 3:00 because she has three therapies a day, all on different days of the week, and it changes from week to week. I have learned to forgive myself when I might not give a 100% of my attention at a feeding because my brain is with the other 500 phone calls and things I need to do today. I have learned to give myself grace. I am not a supermom, and never claimed to be one, but I do love my children and try my best to give 100% that day to whatever needs to be done.

I have also learned to forgive others. I have learned to forgive the person that is old enough not to stare at my daughter because she is different. I have learned to forgive the nurse or doctor who has not read her history and asks if she's always this red or if she's mad or burnt. I have learned to forgive others for their own shortcomings. I have learned to forgive others for not listening to me when I say something I know is right or pertinent to my child's care. I have learned to give others grace.

    4. I have learned that having a "fancy" child is isolating. As much as people try to include you in conversation or act normal around you, they don't. Many are scared to ask you how are things are because they don't know if you want to talk about it, or maybe you'll break down and cry. Many will not talk about their own problems because it is "nothing compared to what Hayley is going through." But here is the truth: I want to know about your child staying up all night because he was teething or she had a fever. I want to know that your child started crawling this week or that she said her first word. I want to know. I want to know because it is life and it makes me feel normal. Even though Millie has a ton of medical issues I am still a mom and I still have stupid mom complaints and I want to be a part of your world. I don't want people to stop talking to me because according to you my life is hard. This makes me feel different and out of place. Please talk to me like I am a normal mom with a normal one year old. She might be different, but don't you worry, I will find something to brag about even if it not the same as your child. I will also let you know when you are complaining too much. I will hopefully let you know in a NICE way that your life is a blessing, and just because your child will not sleep through the night and they are five months old to get over it and be thankful. But on most days, I want to hear about your life. Please let me in.

    5. I have also learned to say YES. I have learned that when people offer something, they truly want to do it—so let them. It makes them feel better and it takes a load off of me. So as much as I want to say "No, please don't bring me breakfast or dinner or mow my grass," I have learned to say "Yes." I have learned that I would do the same if our situations were reversed, and give them the satisfaction and wonderful feeling of doing something for them. Let them ... and then thank them later.

It has been the longest and worst year of my life, but I tell you with all honesty I would not change it for the world. My life might be crazy, disorganized, unusual, full of doctor's appointments and therapies, and painful—but it is also joyful, hopeful, courageous, empowering, and sometimes so filled with love that it feels like my heart might explode, all at the same time. I have been humbled, filled with grace, and loved by others, and it made me realize I am the strongest person I know—all in a year. How many people can say they have learned so much? Not many, and I am thankful that God chose me to be your mom, Millie. Your smile can make me laugh when I fill like crying, your laugh can make a good day bad, your courage and strength can make me feel like I can do anything, and your accomplishments make my heart melt into a puddle of pure excitement. I am so very proud to be your mom. Thank you all for the prayers and support over the years. You will truly never know how it has impacted my life and my family's life. We love you and hope you will continue to love us!!!!

— *Hayley Kolb, Texas*

SWF's Cherished Warrior Mama Behind the Frontlines

by Anne Howard, New Jersey-Editor and writer

When the SWF first came into being, the chief need was for information and emotional support. That has not changed as new families become enmeshed in the new reality of coping with a rare disease diagnosis for their child or for themselves.

But, as we hear from longtime SWF parents, finding the Foundation was a lifeline in a sea of ignorance, misinformation, dire warnings, lack of family empathy, and feelings of isolation and being adrift.

The early Warrior Mamas rose to the challenge and did their homework wherever they could find it. They became the educators of their pediatricians, family doctors, schoolteachers, and families. They grabbed every chance to get involved with early SWF activities, raising funds for programs and materials to spread the word. One mom wrote to the Ann Landers column in her local paper to share the information. Of course, it was picked up nationally and the SWF office had to enlist dozens of volunteers to open and answer the letters (before email or Facebook or Twitter).

There were so many bad things that parents had to contend with; think of the state of laser surgery for one example. Many parents were scared and sad and did not want to face the prospect that their child would have to live with the disfiguration and hypertrophy that untreated Port Wine birthmarks can mean, so the SWF did not use photos with blacked out eyes that the medical texts always used—but instead tried to show and share the accomplishments of kids and adults.

And the Mamas kept up the momentum. Soon the SWF developed regional representatives who would contact each new family in their state and share with them on a personal level, including the names of knowledgeable doctors and practices. And of course, the personal stories of what they had lived through and what they learned stayed with the new families so that—up to this day—you can find SWF families who can remember the first SWF Mama who had reached out to them. The first Day of Awareness grew into Week of Awareness and then the Month. It was started by a Mama. The wrist bands that became so popular in the early 2000s were at the suggestion of a Mama in Michigan.

With the advances in treatments for birthmarks, the SWF encouraged families to get treatment as early as they could; then more doctors became available who were comfortable with and well-equipped to treat PWB. Next, apply that history to seizure meds and surgical treatments. The SWF was and still is a significant prod in the medical community to keep up the battle for more research through membership in professional and governmental organizations. The personal contacts that Karen Ball has made in the past generation have made the difference.

And what of the new parents who come to the SWF after a diagnosis learned in the newborn nursery? They know where to go now. The feelings of isolation and fear may still be there, but there is a wealth of information and empathy that can ease their minds and give them tools for the future.

And what of the kids of those Warrior Mamas? They are living their own lives, now that their parents have done the heavy lifting and prepared the way.

As with all "next generations:" Remember that they didn't watch as seizures happened and changed their future. The present is the only life they know. They don't want to hear any more about what is "wrong" with them; they want to accomplish what they can. The roles are so different for parent and child generally, but the child with a disability does not have the same mindset of the parent. SWS has been part of their whole lives: the doctors, the therapies, the visual differences, the bullying, the social accommodations—and they are still living it.

As adults with SWS gain maturity, perception, and self-knowledge, they are grateful for what their parents did and are still doing. And many of them are happy to participate in SWF activities, coming to conferences, being on committees, running a Facebook page. But the passion of their parents—Warrior Mammas and Dads—is just not there and should not be. Living their own lives is what their parents always worked, hoped, and prayed for. And they are doing it.

Sturge Weber syndrome is only one piece of them. It is not their whole life.

— *Anne Howard, New Jersey-Editor and writer*

(Karen's Two Cents: Anne arrived for her interview to a small conference room crammed with files, desks, and barely anywhere to walk, and she never missed a beat! Our new office was being built and it wasn't ready on time, so—with her sunny can-do, no-worries attitude—I hired her on the spot. For over twenty years, she has been a lifeline for all who need a shoulder to cry on or a roadmap to navigate their life with SWS. She has seen SWS families come and go and employees come and go but remains my beloved Mary Poppins, "practically perfect in every way," and an angel on earth!)

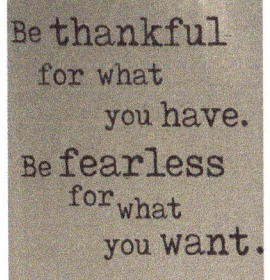
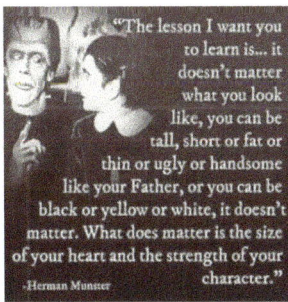

Photo credits: Pinterest.

PART III
ALLIES

CHAPTER 5

The NIH and the FDA

We didn't have much extra revenue in the early years of the SWF to fly to Washington, D.C. to meet with Congress or the National Institutes of Health (NIH). The clinicians were in the early stages of driving clinical care, and with no research funding or an animal model our hands were tied to foster research. I still kept tabs on what research was being done at the NIH in cancer and other vascular malformation diseases who *did* have money to fund research. Eventually, as the donations increased each year, we were able to begin in earnest to advocate for research funding and much more.

The SWF was very lucky that in 1989 Stephen "Steve" Groft became Director of the Office of Rare Disease Research (ORDR) in the Office of the Director at the NIH. The ORDR mission remains to identify, stimulate, coordinate, and support research to respond to the needs of patients with rare diseases. He mentored a staff that mirrored his integrity and passion to improve the lives of patients with a rare disease. The staff's collective curiosity and drive made the SWF mission to fund research and find the cause of Sturge-Weber syndrome so much easier because they have been with us every step of the way—encouraging, partnering, and in many cases acting as a counselor in times of conflict or change.

Danilo "Dan" Tagle, Ph.D. (left), and Steve Groft, Pharm.D.

Steve is a man of integrity and his humbleness inspires all of us to do more for the patients and not our own glory. He retired in 2014 as director of the National Center for Advancing Translational Sciences (NCATS) Office of Rare Diseases Research (ORDR) and has always been a pioneer in the rare disease movement. He had some amazing accomplishments in his career, some of which were supporting research workshops; establishing the Genetic and Rare Diseases Information Center; and establishing the Rare Diseases Clinical Research Network (RDCRN which, by the way, funded SWS research via the Brain Vascular Malformation Consortium). It cannot be stressed enough how much I personally cherish the staff and friends made over the years. You continue to inspire.

Left: Office of Rare Diseases at NCATS; right: Steve Katz, MD.

The National Institutes of Health (NIH)

The National Institutes of Health (NIH) is an immense network of institutes dedicated to improving the quality of life and care for those impacted by diseases. Another institute that had an impact on my own personal learning curve in all things related to basic scientific research was the National Institute for Arthritis, Musculoskeletal, and Skin (NIAMS). The NIAMS Director, Dr. Steve Katz, mentored a staff that also mirrored Dr. Groft's commitment to the patient. Dr. Katz has always sought out ways to bring together the patient's voice and researchers. He instinctively knew this model would drive the pace of discovery. Dr. Katz worked closely with the Coalition of Skin Diseases (CSD, of which I'm a past President and member of the Board of Directors) and forged collaborations which proved fruitful for SWS and birthmarks, pemphigus, alopecia areata, eczema, PXE, and many more skin diseases.

SWF benefited through being able to pick Dr. Katz's brain and also to engage him in presenting and partnering with us to educate Congressional staffers during a Legislative briefing in 2016. This briefing, sponsored by then-U.S. Rep. Ryan Zinke (MT) (and former Secretary of the Interior), gave the SWF exposure to create awareness of our syndrome and placed us in a solid, more competitive position to apply for the third round of funding for the Brain Vascular Malformation Consortium (BVMC) NIH grant. The BVMC funding was critical to the SWS scientists having the necessary funding which enabled us to find the GNAQ gene mutation.

In 2018, I was honored to be nominated by Dr. Katz before his untimely death and appointed to serve on the NIAMS Advisory Council for the 2019–2022 term.

SWF's First Legislative Briefing (2016), sponsored by U.S. Representative Ryan Zinke (MT) (Ret.).

I look forward to giving back any way I can to honor him and his support of the SWF. There are many other institutes at the NIH which are beneficial to the syndrome and the birthmark matters we face every day. It has been an honor to work with all of them to advance patient care and foster research.

We are gearing up in our next strategic phase to work with the Food and Drug Administration's Office of Rare Disease and also the Centers for Disease Control.

Building Blocks

I'm often asked why it takes so long for research. I think it's a lot like building a house. You need a good set of architectural plans, the right builders (scientists and clinicians), and a strong foundation to begin. You can go faster when you have the financial resources (*hint-hint*) and building materials (patients participating and researchers investigating). You can build a lasting legacy of hope for the next generation to take the lead.

The Patient Centered Outcomes Research Institute (PCORI) grant award in 2016 launched a whole new wave of participation by various patients and caregivers. The PCORI funding helped us bring together patients and researchers for the first time and build a team approach to tackling the unknowns of capillary vascular malformations (birthmarks) and SWS.

The NIH not only funds consortiums like our BVMC, which found the cause of SWS, but it also funds the Maryland Brain and Tissue Bank (MBTB). The funding for the MBTB was important for our rare disease because without the funding to procure and store tissue samples, the SWF would not have been able to even start banking tissue. The tissue is critical to launch genetic research studies. Dr. Ronald Zilke was the MBTB Director for many years before he retired, and he was a tireless advocate and friend!

Your tax dollars that support the NIH are so very crucial to driving discoveries which heal not only a body in "DISease," but sad hearts and worried minds too! The NIH is an amazing network of clinicians and scientists who drive innovation and discoveries through strategic collaborations and translational studies. Dr. Francis Collins, NIH Director, has been a long-time champion of rare disease research, and he has been a valued partner in unraveling the mysteries of rare diseases, of which SWS is one of 7,000.

The NIH also has an on-campus hospital for treating patients undergoing, in many cases, a last-ditch effort to find a cure for the unknown medical issues affecting them. They even have an Undiagnosed Institute, where clinicians and scientists really have to turn into investigative sleuths to ferret out a path to health! Their motto should be "no stone left unturned"! *(Karen's Two Cents: Sharon G. was the first woman to publish our newsletters when SWF was in Denver. Sharon contracted mesothelioma many years later. Thanks to my contacts at NIH we were able to get her in a clinical trial on the NIH campus, but sadly lost her way too soon!)*

The U.S. Food and Drug Administration (FDA)

You probably know the FDA exists to protect the public health. They exist to ensure the public can feel safe when they take a prescribed medicine, over-the-counter medicine, or use a product or device. You may not know they also have an Office of New Drugs Rare Diseases Program at the FDA. The office facilitates, supports, and accelerates development of drugs and biologic products for the treatment of patients with rare diseases. The SWF and I got to know the staff over the years at various conferences and meetings. I would listen to their lectures and pick their brains by asking countless questions! The SWF is also a member of the Alliance for a Stronger FDA.

Dr. Marlene Haffner, founding director, and Dr. Tim Cote, former director, were so patient and uplifting in their support and ever hopeful that one day SWS would have new medications to treat our syndrome. *(Karen's Two Cents: Today, Dr. Haffner is retired and has her own consulting company. The SWF is partnering with a new biotech company that is working with Dr. Haffner ... it's a small world!)* The lasers used to treat the birthmark are also reviewed at the FDA.

The SWF is positioning the organization to be ready to partner with industry in getting new medications and devices approved. Organizations are often asked to submit letters of support or testify on behalf of applications, much like for researcher's grant applications at the NIH. The SWF will work with our medical advisors; sometimes we would be able to participate, others maybe not.

Pharmaceutical and Biotech Industry

The pharmaceutical industry has been a vital partner in the SWF's ability to sponsor meetings that bring together key stakeholders to drive clinical and scientific research. They have also partnered with us to sponsor patient meetings, such as the SWF International Family Conference and the Patient Engagement Network (PEN). Hirawats gave the SWF the opportunity to present our first "pitch," which enabled us to identify areas of knowledge to shore up and other ways to tighten the presentation. Immensely helpful as a confidence booster and compass for future directions!

The SWF is a respected organization and as such is asked by pharmaceutical and biotech companies to engage in and to brainstorm potential new studies or treatment indications. It is often the upstart biotech companies that develop a hypothesis and compound to meet a special need and who will then license it to a pharmaceutical company that has a better distribution center and sales force. The SWF has always had short- and long-term goals for partnering with industry as part of our strategic plans. They evolve as we make progress and as new treatments become available.

We are prepared to ensure the next phase of our organizational growth by working with industry-sponsored clinical trials and proceeding with patient recruitments as smoothly as possible, with policies and appropriate consents in place. It's an exciting time for all of us! Please participate whenever and wherever and however you can. You and your family are desperately needed!

CHAPTER 6

Science: Bench to Bedside

I have always heard the saying "bench to bedside" but had no clue what it really all entailed until SWS entered my life! Nor did I understand how long it can take for science and scientists to develop a discovery to the point where it can be used to treat a patient at their bedside. A number of factors and situations have to be in play to increase the pace of discovery in a disease.

For instance, we know it takes dedicated warriors who don't give up and strive to find answers to why their child or they themselves are ill. People will search and find the best and brightest clinicians to treat the illness; sometimes the treatment is a great help, and sometimes, sadly, it's not in time. It takes curiosity, innovative tools, and technology in the hands of intelligent scientists in tandem with new drug discoveries which take years to develop. Collaborators in trusting partnerships brainstorm a hypothesis and design investigations to test them.

Dr. Judah Folkman was one of those rare clinician scientists that never forgot why he conducted research: always what's best for the end user—the

Judah Folkman, MD.

patient! When I first started the SWF, I read an article detailing how he and his lab had just discovered how angiogenesis worked in cancer. It's the process by which a tumor attracts blood vessels to nourish itself and sustain its existence.

So, being an intrepid lil' soul, I called him up! Sure enough, he answered my call and encouraged me to keep thinking in the same vein as to the potential link to angiogenesis and its role in SWS. His humble and down-to-earth demeanor uplifted my spirits and set up for me a lifetime of an ability to not be afraid to ask questions and to find the brightest minds to solve SWS challenges. Furthermore, God was still guiding us! When we had funding to award research grants, we awarded a research grant to German neuropathologist Professor Karl Heinz Plattig. Dr. Plattig's research with tissue samples proved angiogenesis occurs in SWS! Also, not until years later did I learn Dr. Jack Arbiser (who developed the first SWS Murine model) was a fellow in Dr. Folkman's lab! And the choir says, "Amen!"

A key factor in the progress made to develop new treatments is the end user! Patients who participate in clinical trials, donate tissue and blood samples, and who share clinical symptoms are the key drivers with how fast the pace of discovery can happen. Trust me, this bench-to-bedside process can be maddeningly glacial, especially in the rare disease world! Of course, it all takes crucial funding in abundance too.

Dr. Jeffrey Loeb and Dr. Anna Pinto—WARRIORS!

The one area of basic research I hope to see increased in the coming years is in the field of glaucoma. We need to store tissue samples and aqueous humor and match them with clinical data to build a robust catalogue of knowledge. The BVMC and finding the gene was a game-changer. Dr. Jeffrey Loeb and Dr. Doug Marchuk are building a technology platform to create comprehensive and multi-systemic databases linked with clinical data. As enrollment begins, you will see a huge leap in our understanding of SWS and birthmarks.

Dr. Nathan Lawson and Dr. Joyce Bischoff and their labs will also lessen our knowledge gaps with their research utilizing zebrafish and genetics. The identification of new receptors and inhibitors involved in capillary formation and blood flow will create new opportunities for the biotech and drug industries to develop medications to improve the quality of life and care for our loved ones.

Stay tuned and join in the excitement by participating and funding the critical research that's desperately needed to bring answers and hope to the next Warrior Mama and her newborn!

CHAPTER 7

Now What!

Great question! The sky IS the limit and the only thing holding us back is each other. Bold dreams for innovative treatments and cures need bold and diverse funding sources as well as a vast array of volunteers and infrastructure. I believe God has called us to work together to provide the answer to that question.

We each bring unique talents and abilities to assist in fundraising events or networking our circles of influence to fund patient and family support and research. If we don't care enough to participate when we can, how can we expect that anyone not impacted by SWS would care enough? Melanie Wood and Dr. Roy Geronemus were

Left: Dr. John Mulliken; right: Melanie Wood and Dr. Roy Geronemus, SWF Board of Directors Emeritus Members.

and still are leaders doing their part with who and what they know. They came to the fight at key turning points in the Foundation's growth. One person making one commitment truly DOES make a difference. I'm grateful to them both and all of you!

Dr. John Mulliken, Boston Children's Hospital, called one day while I was in the shower. I knew it could be a game changer! So naturally I hopped out of the shower with wet hair dripping and learned that their lab had discovered how capillary malformations occurred. Live in wonder! Show up (oh, OK, dry off first!) and NEVER CEASE TO BE AMAZED!

Still on the Front Lines

I was always taught to lead by example, so it was natural for me to jump right in to solve the unanswered nagging syndrome questions and find medical experts willing to help. There were resources that needed to be identified to minimize the SWS impact on our life and yours. It still amazes me when people just give lip service to "I'm a-gonna" and then, when they have several chances to be men and women of their word, they can't own up to their lack of follow-through or commitment! I KNOW I have high expectations! Yes, not everyone has the calling I have, and the years have mellowed me to a degree. Time is critical and every day we slack off and don't do all we can with what we have, we let down those living with SWS—both on and off the frontlines.

So, I am still on the frontlines with dedicated staff and medical professionals taking up the mantle of this war on Sturge-Weber syndrome. There are more people than ever before engaged on the frontlines raising donations, undertaking research, and lending support-

Julia Terrell, Susan Finnell, and Brian Fisher.

ive hearts and minds. Their commitment gives me more days when I can mentally give myself permission to not feel like I have to "solve" it all by myself. Our lives are richer and more blessed when we invite others to share in the mission and subsequent success.

My personal battleground has also eased up as Kaelin is a young woman able to care for herself. Occasionally, this Warrior Mama is asked to step in and give advice or direction. There have been key difficult moments over the years where Kaelin and I had to establish boundaries to enable her to lead as independent a life as possible. What can I say, but I'm an imperfect mom who loves her daughter more than life itself! Still, I am so proud of her and all we've done for her as well as for all the cherished ones with SWS and birthmarks.

Left: Brian Fisher and Craig Burkhardt, MD; right: Superheroes Grant Fisher and Superman!

All the progress made along the way and the gene discovery was made possible thanks to vital donations. Why wouldn't you donate when you can see all the good that can be done with donations?

I have to be honest: I hate asking for help and donations. Do you hate it too? Plain and simple ... hate it exactly because I don't want to impose on a friendship or feel pitied—but why WOULDN'T you donate when your loved one is living with SWS or your co-worker's child is living with the diagnosis? God wants us to prosper! So, there's always a pep talk rambling around inside my head to just ask, because deep down if you don't ask it just takes longer for God to perform his miracles! I don't want to let Him OR you down! My MOO keeps me grounded and striving to be self-deprecating.

He told me one day, as we were sitting on his deck in Montana and solving world problems, "Kar, did you know there's two ways to spell no?" My ADHD brain, knowing MOO as I do as one who always tries to think positive and drama-free, immediately took it to mean that if someone tells you *no*, flip it so instead of a negative it's a positive *on*, as in game on! But MOO truly meant two ways to spell no: know and no. Sooooo, if someone tells you *no* when you ask for help or donations, you can simply say "Well, I *know* you said *no* but did you mean *no* or *know*—as in let me learn some more to make an informed decision, or to plan when the best time to give will be!" That man is ALWAYS THINKING!

We each have talents to raise critical funds, using our skill set and circle of influence. For instance, some people prefer to just write a check and not roll up their sleeves by hosting a fundraiser. Some like to host events and delight in the details. Other folks work for corporations and they foster grant applications or matching gifts, and others donate stock or leave bequests. The point is ... please do it. Together we are an insurmountable force of nature and DO and WILL make lasting impacts for good.

You've read about some amazing Warriors throughout this book who have contributed as they could. I learned in a Bible study class that God wants us to not just be consumers but also contributors. I'm sure there are times in life where, for a variety of reasons, we just need to be the consumer of wisdom, entertainment, sustenance, etc., but the real bread of life comes in fellowship with one another. The sweetness of life is in contributing ANYWHERE we can to make another's path easier to bear and filled with joy.

It took many years to write this book and publish it. Never really thought what I've done was all that special, just a natural thing any mama would do for her baby. God was always "noodging" though, and is ever faithful!

Pittsburgh, Liberty Boro, Angels in disguise crew raising SWF funds!

CHAPTER 8

How GREAT Thou Art!

I'm shaking my head at how even in the midst of a personal relationship with our Father, I still struggle to Let go and Let God! You either have the mindset that when He answers, you wonder about all the time wasted being so hard-headed, or you go with the flow and say "Amen, yes sir!"

The Holy Spirit has been whispering in my ear for years to take the leap of faith and trust in Him. The man I made a commitment to on August 4, 1984 is a good, good man. We held our marriage together the best we could amidst a war on many fronts, with no idea on which were the next battlefields. In my opinion I imperfectly showed up more than Kirk did, but that is up to our Good Lord to decide.

Of course, by now you know how much commitments mean to our family and why it was so hard to let go of my marriage! There are three entities involved in any union—the two partners and God. We know who's truly in charge in THAT union!

I have immense respect for each man and woman who has gone to war against enemies—foreign or domestic—and especially all rare diseases, including Sturge-Weber syndrome. Only those who have walked in their shoes can truly know the all-encompassing plethora of emotions, struggles, and sweet joys of living the life of sacrifice for the greater good. It forever changes the heart and mettle

Mark "Oz" Geist and Kaelin Ball.

of that warrior and their support system. Forged in steel takes on new meaning!

Similarly, the men and women who go to war to protect our country, our way of life, and their loved ones, will forever be held in my highest regard. Their families also are an integral part of that effort, and their personal casualties—whether on the battlefront or home front—deserve our utmost support. The families impacted by a Sturge-Weber diagnosis or any other rare disease know exactly what I'm talking about. PTSD is a very real result of being on the frontlines too long and seeing too much. Self-confidence, relationships, and much more bear the cost for being courageous warriors. Kaelin had the chance to meet Mark "Oz" Geist, one of the Benghazi heroes, a few years ago and it made me so happy. Two of my most admired and cherished warriors on the planet who conquered and conquer their battles every day with God's help!

Sadly, there will always be war on many battlefronts and for many reasons. The only way I know how to fight them is to honor my family and the code they instilled in us through the generations.

Seeking God's will and turning to Him gives me and I hope you too the ability to maintain and gain strength amidst the battles.

In this next chapter of my life, I have been asking God to hurry up and send me a man of faith, strong in heart and mind, a protector, a nurturer, fiscally responsible, and who has a positive outlook filled with lots of laughter. God was already there, and in His time he brought me out of the desert battleground to another oasis of peace and joy.

Truly out of the blue, God sent just such a warrior. Prefaced with hours of conversations prior to ever meeting face to face, we forged a bond and with a leap of faith slowly built a life. My own Shadow Warrior, Scott, went to war for our country, officials, and corporations where others feared to tread. We both have PTSD moments for different reasons but find common ground of support in our faith and each other.

I feel cherished. I have a partner who encourages me to be all I'm meant to be and to do so with strength, bashful vulnerability,

Ready to rodeo!

and faith. He applauds the journey I have been on since Kaelin was born and can even flip a mean pancake or two with Derek. Lord only knows where we're headed but it will be with humor, joy, and faith. Scott and God truly "have my six," as they say in the military!

Low and behold, the Lord delivered in HIS time, and now every time I sing "How Great Thou Art," the tears fill my eyes in humble gratitude.

May you find reassurance or be uplifted by reading these words. Count your blessings and focus on joy. When we seek joy-filled moments and reactions, I believe they let God's light shine out into the world to light the path of another and ease our own.

Angels in disguise: Colorado Besties always make me laugh and give thanks!

PART IV

TALES FROM THE TRAILS

CHAPTER 9

Tidbits, Tips, and Tales from the Trails

In today's world, it seems many of us can get caught up in the "gottas," "shouldas," and "not yets" in life. You know the hurried state of mind that can keep life from being a fun adventure. Most of us coming from stable homes or homes where we were given a strong foundation intuitively have a sense of adventure and optimism that life has limitless possibilities from childhood onward. Life gets more complicated entering adulthood—or so we can let ourselves be dragged into thinking it is more complicated. MOO reminds us to take it one day at a time and not so seriously because God's looking after us.

For the record, I have to digress here a bit. Daddy doesn't go around talking about God and the impact on his life. He just quietly lives his faith every day and knows who really IS omnipotent, which is what makes us chuckle all the more every time MOO makes a pronouncement!

Stories. Laughter. Tall tales. Laughter. Bullcorn. Laughter. Pathos. Laughter. It just seems that when I look back on my life so far, there has always been laughter. It's not to say there haven't been tears too, but every day there is laughter for one reason or another ... and why not, life is a heck of a lot more fun! MOO *is* a laugh a minute from the moment he gets up in the morning singing, "Good morning to

you, good morning to you, we're all in our places with bright shiny faces, oh this is the way to start a new day," until his head hits the pillow at night, he's taught us to laugh at ourselves and live life in joy because there will always be "doo-doo" to deal with—and that's just a fact of life, too.

Here are a few tidbits, quips, and ditties that never cease to put a smile on our faces, lighten our load, and guide our path in life. Enjoy ... lighten up ... you won't get out of this alive!

Lil' Ditties to Get You Through the Day

It has always been ingrained in us that the Good Lord is in charge and will take care of all your needs. So, thanks to a long generation of irreverent clowns, we have also always had jokes, music, and laughter every day. A day without a good laugh or song bursting forth from our lips or other source is just like a day without sunshine! In the midst of a gloomy or torrentially down-pouring day, we seem to always find something funny—even if it borders on the morbid side (just like many frontline warriors who face death every day).

Here are a few from Mama:

You can do anything you set your mind to!

He IS already there!

Here are a few quips from MOO:

Put a nickel in the drum and you'll be saved.

Dumber than a stump.

Yenom ... Money spelled backwards!

Well, that's the way the cookie crumbles as it rolls down life's crooked road!

What do you think of the rectum as a hole ... it's a dirty crack!

Do your ears hang low, do they wobble to and fro, do your ears hang low: *"Long fellow."*

MOO on Work ...

This is something he always says when we'd get frustrated or life was becoming overwhelming: Plan your work and work your plan. (Imagine a cartoon character with highly sharpened pencil on the tip of his tongue with balloon over his head with a running list.)

Load the wagon! (Visions of man with cartoon balloons surrounding his head with scenes from a life of LOAD THE WAGON: bills, bills, bills; a bad boss; a nagging wife; screaming kids; water-filled kitchen from broken dishwasher; etc.)

He's so dumb he couldn't pour water from a boot with the instructions written on the heel!

When you retire ... you're not the lead dog anymore but the fire hydrant.

MOO on Home and Family ...

Hello, is this the party to whom I'm speaking ...

Nothing good happens after midnight, MOO Speaks!

MOO on Life ...

If you have ever seen hogs at the trough when the slop has just been put in, you can really visualize where this one came from: MOO always used it to basically say: "Well, what you gonna do is get down to ... Root Hog or Die."

Hobo rides on a boxcar ... *"Long fellow"*

The body got fed and the belly button says, "What do I do with the stuff down below me?" The tummy says to the bummy, "Bombs away!"

Musings and Tales from the Warrior Mama

I can honestly say that thanks to my parent's genuine love to be with each other—and love *for* each other through good times and bad—our family has had a solid foundation to feel secure and loved. They inherited that same foundation from their parent's generation to the next generation. I like to think I'm quick-witted and funny too, but alas, when we all get together it is like an unspoken rivalry to see who can crack the first joke or bullcorn to make everyone laugh!

Truthfully, while I am not the funniest or most eloquent of writers—or the most grammatically correct—I have tried to listen for when the Holy Spirit tells me to pick up my pen or rattle the keyboard and take down his notes! Here are a few blogs and articles written through the years that I hope will resonate with you and provide some inspiration:

They Said!

They Said: You've got your hands full with a sick baby; you can't start an organization. (Fundraising Totals: 1987=$0; 2019=$813,000)

They Said: You're working and raising a handicapped child; you shouldn't add a fundraiser to your plate too. (Pennsylvania proud for twenty-five years)

They Said: Stick with softball, it's what you know—but a Gala was born. (Houston proud)

They Said: You're too rare for corporate pharma to support you. (Reunion of Champions Lead On)

They Said: You started with a cookbook and moved on to a Road race—just don't tackle too much. ($1,000,000 total raised in ten years)

They Said: You'll never find the gene that causes SWS because it's not inherited. (Brain Vascular Malformation Consortium-GNAQ gene mutation)

They Said: This new generation of millennials needs a medal. (Indiana, Illinois, Texas, and more—Warriors Deliver)

They Said: There's a lot of competition out there for researchers to find a cure. (Mouse and Zebrafish make a splash!)

They Said: Clinical trials are way off. (CBD trials 2019, Glaucoma trials 2020)

WE SAID: Believe ... and we WILL make an impact!

We've all heard people use the phrase often enough, "Yeah, but THEY SAID...." It's as if the person making the pronouncement—just by the sheer fact that they are stating it—makes whatever they are commenting on a truth or a done deal! Really ... come on. I've always been one who, when I hear that phrase, immediately revert to "Well, watch this!"—unless of course it's from an admired source who is your own personal cheerleader and "They Said: You can do whatever you set your mind to!"

I'm happy to report I've been fortunate to be surrounded by others of the same mindset! Which in turn means you are fortunate too, because without them the SWF would not have made all the strides we have since 1987.

Heal Your Heart and Heal Your Head!

I started thinking about the head and heart while at an American Academy of Dermatology AADA event. I pondered the difference between the older generation and the millennial generation after almost thirty-two years of leading the SWS and SWF battle while cheering families and researchers on and sometimes being a shoulder to cry on. I noticed at the meeting there was a mix of older and younger advocates and physicians. In many respects we are alike: our devotion to being treated or treating patients with respect and our commitment to finding financial and legislative solutions to the various diseases we are dedicated to conquering. I believe in any generation there is a generalization for the work ethics and moral values that epitomizes each one. I also believe there are the outliers that define or change the shift from one generation to the next.

Specifically, in Sturge-Weber syndrome there has been the shift in support and networking people. In 1987, SWF started with an all-volunteer support system with expensive long-distance phone calls (or snail mail!). In 2021, staff and volunteers are developing content to get information from websites, and today the expectation is that there should be an immediate reply or access to information 24/7/365. The older generation *in general* has been conditioned to have self-reliance and to do their own sleuthing and communication to obtain necessary care and knowledge. They also are more comfortable visiting in person rather than relying on technology to communicate. It makes their lives sometimes harder and slower, but they don't impose on others to do their heavy lifting. The millennials *in general* expect that discomfort and fear need to be "fixed" ASAP, and it's up to someone else to deal with what they need, when they need it, and how they need to receive it and make it easy to enable them to deal. Take a deep breath; I'm not dashing the Greatest Generation nor bashing millennials—I'm simply stating the generalizations of the two generations. I am lucky to have met and to know some AMAZING millennials and older generations as well as their outliers in both generations!

The level of support and manpower required to meet the emerging 24/7/365 needs of a new generation of patients was taken into consideration at the Board of Director's recent Strategic Planning Retreat. For example, one volunteer thinks websites are basically old school and the suggestion was to repost information and video medical lectures on Facebook and other social media platforms. Great idea... you *can* teach an old dog new tricks! Another volunteer prefers to know ALL the back story first.

Patience and open communication are key attributes needed between generations—not only in a relationship, but with your healthcare providers, school officials, employers, etc. There is no wrong or right way to accomplish this, because as you know there are people who like bulleted talking points vs. narrative written materials, and people who like curves and people who like angles. Our goal as the SWF volunteers and staff is to give it our best effort to create learning materials that meet diverse learning styles, medical needs, cultural differences, and so much more ... and yes, to generate enough revenue to maintain programs and access at your fingertips. We aim to please. We appreciate your participation and financial support. We appreciate your patience and understanding in our service and your reception of those services.

On a personal level, it is our personal responsibility to heal our own heart and head. No one else or no organization or healthcare provider can do that for you. You know yourself best and you need to BE at your best to bring a strong advocate to lead the charge for your loved one with SWS. We also have to be cognizant of what our intent and tone are implying and saying, whether online or in person. Respect for and tolerance of another opinion or experience is tantamount to safeguarding vulnerable recipients and less-knowledgeable providers.

The fight or flight emotions rear their heads at the most inopportune times, which is why it's best to plan your work and work your plan, as ol' MOO says. Sure, plans go awry—so you need a backup plan, and another backup plan, and *another* backup plan! The wealth of wisdom among the generations is your treasure for healing your heart and head. Take advantage of their wisdom as well as their experiences, and be sure to leave some for the next generation by being open minded, present, and having a presence online or in person. I know you'll make the right decision to heal your heart and head in whichever particular order fits you best. We'll forgive each other our unintended transgressions because our mutual goal for our loved ones is the same: quality of life, and care and a cure!

Nothing Good Happens After 12 Midnight OR 12 Noon!

I saw that wink! The words were out of my mouth before I knew what I was saying ... my, how the tables have turned! My Mama had winked at MOO when I was discussing their ability to drive later in the day and the need to be careful on the road at ninety-one years of age.

When I was growing up, my dad, aka MOO—Mighty Omnipotent One, used to tell us ALL the time nothing good happens after midnight! Our curfew was midnight and woe unto you if you missed the deadline. For the most part, I was a good lil' girl and complied 'cuz I love my Daddy beyond measure, and the silence that would follow an infraction of the rules was more hurtful than the punishment ... I'd let myself down. In his quiet and stalwart way, he was teaching us self-respect for self AND others. The action/decision reinforcing it was bad, not the person. Of course, as a veteran mom, I now recognize they would lay awake until we got home, safely knowing there were all kinds of things that could happen to us even if we were not at fault. Whether you are a parent of a special needs child and you worry about medical issues, financial issues, or family relationships, or simply a parent with everyday issues (or one who juggles them all)—at the heart of it is love. Firsthand experience tells me that when you juggle special-needs-times-two kids and you're senior parents, the love and need to nurture the self is even more critical!

I happened to have parents who by sheer force of will on some occasions were gonna make us tow the mark or ELSE. Every family has stories that get regaled and embellished over the years, but the love is always there in the telling! I ramble on about this part of my life because while you are in the midst of raising your child with SWS and their siblings, you are worrying and celebrating from both sides of the parenting aisle. It hit me when I was flying home from a recent visit to Montana with Mama 'n' Daddy that when I said those words, "I saw that wink," the tables had truly been turned and that lil' karma as THEY say can be a force to be reckoned with, to be sure.

It's not easy being a parent ... can't be faint of heart if you want to raise a respectable adult who won't be a burden on the family or society. It takes lots of planning. It's even harder when raising a child with a rare disease like SWS—so many unknowns! I struggled about Kaelin between worry and faith every step of the way and still do today, much as my parents probably did and do for me—but let's face it, worry is a wasted emotion and shows a lack of faith. There is always a balancing act of empowering your child(ren) to have the best quality of life and independence they can while ensuring they maintain self-respect and safety in and out of the home. This doesn't change at any development stage or age!

So, with my Mama's lil' wink to Daddy about driving somewhere I thought they shouldn't, I made a decision and decided nothing good happens after 12 Noon! If it was good enough for them to not worry, it's good enough for me too. The deeper the love for someone, the "letting go" becomes so much harder, whether handing the keys to your new teenage driver, coming to grips with the path your SWS diagnosis has taken, or preparing yourself to say the final goodbye to the only parents and compass(es) you have known who will always love you unconditionally!

Planning and communication are key whether you are raising a child—special needs or otherwise—or planning for your parents' age-related issues. I urge you to take time annually to check in with your spouse and children to say, "How we doing?" Seek outside input too. Say "I love you" every day in every way! Exhale. In the blink of an eye, you will look back and marvel at how you got here.

I love you every day in every way ... with faith, hope, and love,
Karen

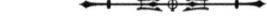

Carry Your Water ...

This summer in Colorado we have been hit really hard by wildfires. First, my brother had to evacuate his home during one fire. It was a truly sobering reminder that what is important is not the stuff, but sitting with him savoring a good scotch and swapping war stories! Then, as I was watching the smoke billow up over the peaks behind the house due to the Weston Pass fire, I realized our lives with SWS and birthmarks are similar to these fires. We have to have a plan and be prepared for the unexpected. We never know when the winds of change will whip up and carry us in a direction that wasn't on our radar or even the map!

I can now take the wait-and-see approach, as opposed to holding my breath and being ever-ready to run, after over thirty-four years of dealing with Kaelin's challenges! That attitude doesn't mean we don't have a plan and aren't prepared for all the "What ifs" that are surely ahead. It means that, like the wildfire season in Colorado, you learn to accept the things that are out of your control. You learn to savor every beautiful sunrise and sunset when your kids are giggling or trying to catch fireflies. You learn ... this too shall pass.

I encourage you to explore new vistas and dream BIG dreams for your child, yourself, and your family. If you had told me when Kaelin was a baby that I'd be sitting here typing this article with a planned $1,000,000-plus budget for next year, I probably would have taken a BIG gulp and said BRING IT ON! My dreams for her, myself, and our family—which includes you—WERE and ARE bigger! So many dreams, so little time! My dad says "Kar, the only time you fail is when you don't get back up!" Well, this Warrior Mama won't let any fire or budgetary challenge put me out. I put THEM out! I know you have that spark inside you too.

It is our duty to bring every bucket of water and tool we have in our arsenal to put out the pesky lil' fires of worry, fear, doubt, and more, before they rage into paralyzing infernos. It's okay to spend some time managing them by "carrying your water," a.k.a. taking time to just chill, to let life ebb and flow around you ... this too shall pass. Of course, when our lives do hit those times when a wildfire whips up around us through seizures, ischemic strokes, eye surgeries, or even worse, a brain surgery—exhale and carry out your plans. Can you tell I was a good Girl Scout and Campfire Girl?! Seriously, remember to include in your plan joy and laughter; it's the balm that soothes amidst times of trouble.

Happy rest of the summer ... can't wait to see the vacation photos of Webster on the road or just y'all chilling! With faith, hope, and love, Karen

The Path You Have Been Given

The path you have been given will not be easy. It will require you to have your eyes wide open. It will need you to be nimble and adapt to change. This path will cause you to needlessly worry when you stumble or maybe even fall. Your heart and desire WILL be tested.

Exhale. Be present. Enjoy the view!

The beauty that surrounds you is like no other. Cherish the easy and rugged parts of your path, for each one enriches the moment. They leave a lasting imprint on your heart and inspire those around you. You are one of life's greatest guides.

Know that with every step forward AND step backwards, you ARE making strides that leave a lasting impact on you and those who travel with you. Give yourself permission to be vulnerable and to revel in every success and celebration, no matter how small. Your path is not the way of the masses. It requires courage, faith, hope, and love.

I believe you have it in you to illuminate your way by sharing your joy and pain with those you meet along the way. There will be people with wisdom who have walked the same path and saw different sites than you, or have equally vulnerable knowledge to share. Embrace each viewpoint and gather each spark; they ignite and make your life a shining example of what tenacity in the face of adversity can do!

You are strong. You are wise. You matter. You are beautifully made. There is only one you, and I believe you will overcome and prevail. In no time at all, you will reach the final destination and look back and say to yourself, "I forged ahead and never stayed down. I had amazing guides, and I reached back, and I gave a spark of hope to those behind me ... that was enough." Rest and be in peace!

In loving memory of Noel Gelfund, Chad Layman, and Paul Siegel

Just Remember ...

Success is not final and failure is not fatal; it is the courage to continue that counts. — *Winston Churchill*

Just remember, God gives you the most strength when you are at your weakest point. — *Battle Ready a Warrior Medic*

Just remember, if you do the right things for the right reasons, the right people will know it and the right people you try to reach will have better lives because of it. That's why God gave you that cross to bear, not the navy; His son bore a cross too, you know. — *Unknown*

In the end we are all separate: Our stories, no matter how similar, come to a fork and diverge. We are drawn to each other because of our similarities, but it is our differences we must learn to respect. — *Johann Wolfgang von Goethe*

You are today where your thoughts have brought you; you will be tomorrow where your thoughts take you. — *James Allen*

You can't plan a winning strategy if you can't define winning. — *Unknown*

Self-inflicted isolation ... what are the effects of it vs. importance of engaging with SWF ... no one should ever feel their alliance with SWF ends when the crisis is over or the world is righted once again ... helping families transition from crisis phases to "normal" and back again can help a person a great deal.

Trust is the most essential element of someone seeking assistance ... but you must be amenable to talk about the dark side too.

I can never get back the years I was traveling or numbing my stressors and emotionally separating. I hope that one day all of you will come to understand that the ravages of war are inevitable, and the cost of bearing that banner is high but noble and oh so worth it—and to know I wish I could have been more of a June Cleaver kind of mama. God called and I answered, and I hope one day you can listen and answer your own call.

The ALS Ice Bucket challenge is all the rage now and for good reason. In 1939, New York Yankees baseball star Lou Gehrig was struck down in his prime with this neurological disorder, which made it so devastating and still resonates with the public today. For those living with this devastating disease, we are so glad that the public supports them.

The bucket challenge got me to thinking how this happened and why so few clamor to our SWS cause. Here's my Two Cents ... ALS and baseball are more relatable and thus more personal. You think, "One can go along with expectations that all will be well until one day ALS strikes and you are no longer in control and life will never be the same." Do you suppose an acquired disease creates more sympathy from the public than one you are born with? (Again, the "Oh Lord, that could be me" vs. the "Oh Lord, that's so sad and I'm glad it's not me" thinking.) Either way, ill health (*DIS-ease*) is a chilling reminder that life is to be cherished every day and is fleeting. For those of us in the dugout waiting our turn on deck, that's a no brainer!

The opportunity to be a Champion for a fellow life-traveler is waiting for you. I'm strong, I'll lift this for you, and the world can see I'm a caring person too. Lou Gehrig didn't start out life with any strikes against him—he lived a full life and even played baseball for the New York Yankees.

I love that the challenge showed the power of ONE! For years, I've been saying "just do one thing—ANYTHING—but just do it." One donation, one kind deed for those families coping every day with SWS, one bumper sticker on your car, attending (or better yet) hosting a fundraiser, calling your representative to increase National Institute of Health funding ... one thing WILL make a world of difference! We too are building a Circle of Friends and Champions that CAN and MUST rival their challenge!

Y'all know about my lifelong Champions for Danny in McKeesport, Pennsylvania, and for twenty-five years they said "Batter up!" and held events that raised critical funds and hit one out of the ballpark for SWF and Danny. We almost lost Danny ... now in an induced coma, struggling to keep an airway open because of the tissue overgrowth in his throat. Our little thirty-one-year-old Irish inspiration had more than three strikes against him from birth, but his grit pulled him through once again. Finding the GNAQ gene was just one hit in the game ... Danny is waiting for our home run that will win the game!

We have a new Champion for a Cure. His name is Will. He is twelve years old and he lives the power of one every day! He held his first Carnival for a Cause event this summer and raised $5,600

... twelve years old. The circle of friends that participated had a fun day and supported an amazing young man who cares deeply about a little girl with SWS, Stella. With his "one thing," he's betting that he'll hit a home run for her and all of us. I believe it's possible because every dollar we raise brings us closer to the cure, through partnering with biotech companies, developing targeted therapies, and conducting clinical trials.

The SWF Board of Directors will meet this Fall to set bold and achievable new strategic goals. We need you to please challenge yourself for TEAMSWF. I thank you for donating and as a team player we need you now more than ever! I challenge you to step up to the plate like McKeesport, Pennsylvania, did for Danny and Will did for Stella. Make the clutch play by increasing your gift today! Are you up to the challenge?

With faith, hope, and love, Karen

Since this was first written, Danny has passed away and Will has gone on to help another young girl in need of support.

The Victim or the Victor?

Choice. It's all about choice and discipline with a sprinkle of nurture. We've all read about people and even know people that have overcome insurmountable odds in life that could have made the individual a failure. I've always been curious about the impact one kind word or a word of encouragement can have on an individual's life course. My wise old dad, MOO (Mighty Omnipotent One), always said that if you didn't get a child by the time they were six, the die is cast.

I'm realizing now that he meant knowing right from wrong. One can always gain more education and obtain new skill sets to improve your lot in life. One can seek out mentors to guide us in building worthy, impactful lives, and which remind us of our worth. Without a good moral compass though, an individual may miss out on many opportunities! I taught school before I had Kaelin. I always tried to instill in my kids that they were unique and worthy and no one else was like them. Some of their parents were extremely strict, some extremely lax, and of course there were those in the middle—but having an outside validation of their self-worth was always wanted and needed.

When you're dealing with a progressive rare disease, there are days—OK, *many* days—when one can feel like a victim without the energy to get up and continue on, because life is just too hard and too expensive and just plain unfair! The whole circle of comparison between "Your child is higher functioning than mine" or "Your child walks and mine doesn't" or "Your child's birthmark is less than mine" is a spiral that has no good resolution—nor does it imbibe confidence in your child that they can be victorious! One must be vigilant against staying a victim. It takes discipline, but I believe you and our children with SWS deserve the very best of us and they deserve nothing less than as much victory as we can provide and imbibe!

My Gramma's Chairs ... Celebrating Life, Loss, and the Faith That Sees Us Through It

My Gramma's Chairs have solid wood frames with a curving inset panel and a padded seat meant to be reupholstered. My Mama and Daddy arranged the transfer of stewardship of those chairs after my Gramma Fisher passed away. I was a young wife and mama with a beautiful baby girl and little money. The chairs weren't enamel when I became their steward. They were good, solid chairs bought at a bargain, I surmise. I often gaze upon the black enamel upright dining room chairs with nostalgia and gratitude. The filigreed inset lends some elegance to my humble home. I remember family and friends sitting on those seats sharing tales of laughter, joy, and shaggy dog stories that never ended. I recall tales of frustration, anger, and loss, usually intermingled with my tears spilled forth. There has been loss much too soon and loved ones still dearly missed. Gramma's chairs remind me where I come from and what's important in life. The chairs are more often empty today than filled with family since we are in New Jersey, but they still whisper to me as if to say, "Don't worry, we're here with another seat ready for the taking and another tale to tell!"

My Gramma Fisher lived through early years of happy times, raising five children and loving a traveling salesman. The chairs were moved from Susanville, California, to Helena, Montana, where he worked a new territory and she maintained the home front during the Great Depression. From his letters, Grampa Fisher loved her deeply and cherished her throughout his life. He is one of those cherished ones I mentioned who died too soon. Pneumonia, the doctors said—and their lives were forever changed. I can only imagine what those chairs were privy to hear as my Daddy and family sat around the table to absorb the shock of the loss. I've heard tales that Daddy used to keep Gramma company while she crocheted the beautiful doilies that grace my house today. Self-reliance to make not purchase what household items a family needed.

Gramma was a good home-cookin,' rib-stickin' type of cook. The boys would go out and hunt down deer, pheasant, and fish and she'd fry 'em up in some bacon grease to mouthwatering perfection. I can't help but reflect that back then in Montana (and still today) there was nothing strange about going into the wild to get your food vs. the aisle of the local food store ... especially if you were on a fixed income. Can't you imagine the tales the boys had to tell around that dining room table, rocking back on the chairs, with each tale getting more outrageous and boastful about feats of valor in the hunt! Laughter and joy amidst life's challenges which struck again when the second oldest son was shot by accident with a shotgun and it took out part of his lung ... no health insurance and a long hospital stay ... another bill to pay. Gramma didn't rely on the government to pay her bills ... the kids all held jobs and contributed, and my cherished chairs were filled with tales of the day's toil, labors, and tips. World War II saw Gramma's eldest son enlist in the Navy and the chairs must have had her sitting for hours on end writing letters (remember those!) as he served on the high seas in Pearl Harbor … worry filled those chairs during those years, and faith too! Work. Work. Work. Work was all their generation knew, along with self-reliance and faith.

Life rolled along. The chairs began to hold tales from family additions as spouses were added and grandchildren flourished. Gramma worked for the State of Montana after Grampa Fisher passed away, and then worked at the old people's center until she retired in her late eighties. Life continued to bring further tough times as two granddaughters were diagnosed with cancer, one committed suicide (another loss too soon), one was born with a rare disease, and Gramma eventually succumbed to a stroke. As they broke down her home, Daddy rescued the chairs for me. At the time, I only had an English pub table in the dining room and the chairs would be a welcome addition to our first home.

On one hand, Lord knows I've longed to buy REAL dining room chairs and table for the dining room, but life had other plans and bills to pay. On the other hand, the chairs and I keep a tether to a rich, family-filled past honoring sorrows, sacrifices, and celebrations. The chairs and I have stories to tell and I don't care if others may look upon my chairs as old tattered 'less than' additions to my home. They remind me of what's important in life: people not things. They remind me to cherish those who occupy the seats at my table and the Mama who taught me to recycle and refurbish. My Mama is the queen of decorating on a budget, so it stood to reason by example that when I changed my décor the chairs naturally would change too! Some psychologist would have a field day with the symbolism of what the painted and chipped chairs reveal!

The first color I see peeking through the various chipped areas is a rosy red … reflecting the hope of a bright future. I remember painting them in between my baby girl's naps. I was being thrifty as a proud stay-at-home mom. I slipcovered the seats too—staple by staple, proud as could be for my clumsy efforts. Rosy red to complement the carpet my brother shipped to us. The painting allowed me to focus creatively during a time of what I thought was great worry … too bad I never learned to crochet! It was the beginning of an adventure the chairs and I would share for a lifetime. With a Sturge-Weber diagnosis at birth, my baby had three eye surgeries in her first three months of life and seizures at a year. Sturge-Weber stalks us even today and we've laughed in the face of adversity and solved weighty problems at the table, shifting around in those chairs. I've celebrated milestones I never thought would be reached and we've laughed at each other as we try to snag the win during table games.

Life rolled along. The chairs moved with us across country to New Jersey. I followed my husband, much as my Gramma Fisher did with her husband, and we settled into a new life. Our daughter was flourishing in spite of the diagnosis and our newborn son—with as-yet undiagnosed—autism promised to keep life lively. Naturally, a fixer-upper home required new décor to ease the tears and fears I had at leaving beloved family and cherished friends. The solid, dark green spray paint replaced the hopeful rosy red. Busy life transitions from stay-at-home mom to full-time working mom coincided with active school-age children and travel schedules. The chairs' new coat of paint made me feel safe and cocooned during years of joy at seeing my children grow into uplifting gifts and weathering intermittent turmoils that seemed unendurable. My Gramma's chairs ... if she could survive and thrive, so could I.

Life rolled along. Birthdays, graduations, illness, and surgeries—the chairs and I have had our share of tales to tell and to listen to over the years. They continue to remind me that a solid foundation and family history can see us through anything in life. I suspect my daughter doesn't cherish these chairs now as I do, but I hope one day she'll know why they mean so much to me.

The chairs got shipped one more time back to Colorado in 2015. The pub table has been replaced with a beautiful black enamel hand-painted barn table. The chairs need a new coat of paint and to be reupholstered. Haven't quite figured out why I didn't dive right in and do it once we were settled. I surmise to a great degree I'm settled. Life will go on and it has been a GREAT blessing!

Angels Among Us!

"I only know the names of two angels! Hark and Harold." — *Gregory, age five*

"Everybody's got it all wrong. Angels don't wear halos anymore. I forget why, but scientists are working on it." — *Olive, age nine*

"It's not easy to become an angel! First, you die. Then you go to heaven; then there's still the flight training to go through. And then you got to agree to wear those angel clothes." — *Matthew, age nine*

"Angels work for God and watch over kids when God has to go do something else." — *Mitchell, age seven*

"My guardian angel helps me with math, but he's not much good for science." — *Henry, age eight*

"Angels don't eat, but they drink milk from holy cows." — *Jack, age six*

"Angels talk all the way while they're flying you up to heaven. The basic message is where you went wrong before you got dead." — *Daniel, age nine*

"When an angel gets mad, he takes a deep breath and counts to ten. And when he lets out his breath, somewhere there's a tornado." — *Reagan, age ten*

"Angels have a lot to do and they keep very busy. If you lose a tooth, an angel comes in through your window and leaves money under your pillow. Then when it gets cold, angels go north for the winter." — *Sara, age six*

"Angels live in cloud houses made by God and his son, who's a very good carpenter." — *Jared, age eight*

"All angels are girls because they gotta wear dresses, and boys didn't go for it." — *Antonio, age nine*

"My angel is my grandma who died last year. She got a big head start on helping me while she was still down here on earth." — *Katelynn, age nine*

"Some of the angels are in charge of helping heal sick animals and pets. And if they don't make the animals get better, they help the kid get over it." — *Vicki, age eight*

"What I don't get about angels is why, when someone is in love, they shoot arrows at them." — *Sarah, age seven*

> *If God brings you to it, He will bring you through it.*
> *Happy moments, praise God.*
> *Difficult moments, seek God.*
> *Quiet moments, worship God.*
> *Painful moments, trust God.*
> *Every moment, thank God.*
>
> by Lottie McDonald

Lessons from Geese

Next time you see geese heading south for the winter, flying along in the V-formation, you might be interested in knowing what science has discovered about why they fly that way.

It has been learned that as each bird flaps its wings, it creates an uplift for the bird immediately following. By flying in V-formation, the whole flock adds at least seventy-one percent greater flying range than if each bird flew on its own.

Lesson: People who share common direction and sense of purpose can get there quicker and easier because they are traveling on the thrust of one another.

Whenever a goose falls out of formation, it suddenly feels the drag and resistance of trying to go it alone and quickly gets back into formation to take advantage of the lifting power of the bird in front of it.

Lesson: It's harder to do something alone than together. If we have as much sense as a goose, we stay in formation with those headed where we want to go. We are willing to accept their help and give help to others.

When the lead goose gets tired, it rotates back in the wing and another goose flies into point position.

Lesson: Shared leadership and interdependence gives us each a chance to lead as well as opportunities to rest. Also, it pays to take turns doing the hard tasks and sharing leadership. As with geese, people are interdependent on each other's skills, capabilities, and unique arrangements of gifts, talents, or resources.

The geese in formation honk from behind to encourage those up front to keep up their speed.

Lesson: We need to make sure our honking is encouraging. In groups where there is encouragement, the production is much greater. The power of encouragement (to stand by one's heart of core values and encourage the heart and core of others) is the quality of honking we seek.

When a goose gets sick or wounded by gunshot or falls out, two geese fall out of formation and follow it down to help and protect it. They stay with the goose until it is able to fly or until it is dead; and then launch out on their own or with another formation to catch up with their original group.

Lesson: Stand by your colleagues in difficult times as well as in good. If we have as much sense as geese, we will stand by each other in difficult times as well as when we are strong.

You see, all we have to do to attract those who are not participating is to demonstrate to the world that we have as much sense as geese. That seems like a small enough price to pay to win the lost and help one another.

SpringHill Suites ... in a hotel room all alone, or home alone in a house full of people ... is that the place labeled lonely? The years of travel and being away from family can and often do take a toll on everyone. I had this question pop into my head in the SpringHill Suites in Atlanta while attending yet another conference ... having a lil' pity party on the bed before meeting a local family. It was a heart-wrenching time in our life and I had to suck it up buttercup, BIG time, to go down and put on a happy face. I decided to order room service before I went down to the lobby.

There was a knock on the door and the food was delivered. I'll never forget this moment: as the room service woman was turning to leave the room, she turned around and said, "I'm supposed to tell you all will be well have faith. God has a plan." Shocked was an *understatement!* By now, I'd begun to know that God sends angels to us and I was so thankful to have received the message. Here's the best part though! I went down and met the family and shared with them the amazing moment with room service. It was a very healing moment, where we, as Warrior Mamas, shared our joys and pains and our faith that binds the wounds and wipes the tears and eases the fears. God does work in mysterious ways!

Just gotta keep showing up and have faith and he'll do the rest!

WEEDS ... Gotta Love 'em!

I am a person who for the record HATES weeds! It seems I've been having to do A LOT of weeding lately, both personally and in the yard. In the course of pulling or spraying the insidious lil' suckers, it gives me and you lots of time to think about the landscape of our life and property.

For instance, on the literal level, let's face it, if you don't stay a step ahead of those pesky invading weeds, they will literally take over your lawn, garden, and—in my case—cracks in the driveway. Oh, I could run with the weeds in the cracks analogy, but I won't digress! I have come to conclude the reason weeds bug me so much is because I have always been a person to focus on the joy and beauty in life. Be present to what is right in front of you. Attend to what has gone awry before it gets worse. Don't let one aspect of SWS etc. choke out the good times. Nurturing good feelings, whether giving or receiving them, has always been at the core of my being, and when I have to focus on the irritating "weeds," it annoys me and slows me down. Attending to the weeds forces me to focus on one area rather than the whole landscape ... 'course, maybe that's the purpose!

In relation to Sturge-Weber syndrome, Klippel-Trenaunay syndrome, and Port Wine birthmarks, our proverbial weeds creep in when we do not take care of ourselves physically and mentally. Taking your medication on time and making those appointments to get laser treatments for the birthmark is imperative to keeping your "landscape" nourished and flourishing. Be mindful of when you are getting dehydrated, too tired, or stressed, and take time to recharge your batteries. It is so important—so you can maintain a healthy outlook on life to the best of your ability. Exercise is also key to a healthy body AND MIND! Loathe as I am to admit it, as I fight to take back my marshmallow-like body, to one of a lean, mean, fighting machine.... I DO feel better after I get out in nature and walk. Yep, I get to see the weeds people are not attending to in their yards—but I get to see the beautiful gardens of those folks who are mindful, too.

Let's face it, whether it's our physical landscape or our beautiful bodies, we only have one at a time. Give yourself a break when you slip or slide in maintaining either one, but don't stay down! Your assets are worth the effort and you'll feel a sense of accomplishment for having maintained them. I feel that way about the Sturge-Weber Foundation.

I am proud of how all of you have nurtured the programs and research with your time, talents, and treasure. I appreciate all the volunteers who with us attend to our weeds by doing tasks that NEED to be done—but we rarely get time to do them! I'm excited to walk with everyone in our annual *Routes to a Cure* walk and cheer on those of you who are doing local walks or virtual walks online. Every mile and every penny raised keep the weeds at bay and nurture vital programs that serve so many in need.

Here's to the dog days of summer, when we toil in the hot weather to keep the weeds at bay so we can enjoy the playtime so richly deserved after all our hard labors!

Roadblocks to Rescue

I first heard about roadblocks from Scott, my cherished last love, after a men's meeting at our Clearview Church in Buena Vista, Colorado. I suppose as a Methodist I'd heard a sermon or two over the years that mentioned how God puts up roadblocks for our own good, but truthfully, as a child I was probably not listening and instead ruminating over what kind of tasty treats there would be during coffee hour! I have to say that I'm more enlightened today than at any

Sometimes God will put a Goliath in your life, for you to find the David within you

other time in my life. There were so many times that I thought a *no* answer or *no* from God was punishment. My loving heavenly Father was really protecting me and guiding me to where he needed me to go. WOW! Who knew!?! "Ye of little faith" is ringing in my ears!

I got to wondering about roadblocks in my own life and also in my family tree. Why do they hurt so much? So why give me free will if you're just gonna put a roadblock up? Of course, in the reveal of time I got it and get it and how much easier life would be if I just had prayed and let God! There have been some "noodges" and some whoppers that I pray never to repeat. All of them have made me dig deeper in my faith and trust. I am where I am today because of Him. The family examples of how to cope with grace in the face of adversity are numerous and were also influential factors. Here are just a few highlights from the family tree:

My family tree is riddled with roadblocks to rescue and turn messes into messages! My Gramma Fisher had one heck of a roadblock when her young husband died and left her with no income, no insurance, and five young children to raise! My Gramma Lou had some whopper roadblocks too! She was quarantined at home with her first young child who had scarlet fever; her young husband died, leaving her with three young children to raise; then she moved into her brother's home, went to work, and I'm sure you recall the rest of her story from earlier tales!

The point is we ALL have roadblocks that might not be as big as my Grammas' roadblocks were, but our faith is surely tested. How we navigate them depends on whether we are rescued from a path or circumstance in life or keep repeating the same steps.

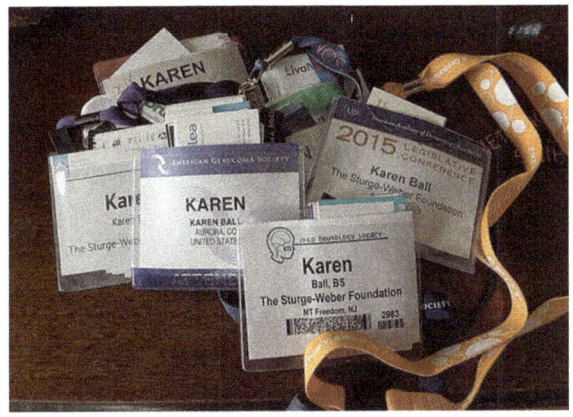

I'm a Lanyard Lover … and I Give Thanks!

If you multiply one event lanyard times twelve to fifteen events a year, times thirty-four years … well, you do the math! Each tag represents not only a moment in time that helped me learn more and cherish long-time friendships anew, but brought a deep sense of gratitude for the life I've been given and am living.

'Course, there were times gratitude was sorely tested because I'd get so tired and ticked off that Sturge-Weber syndrome had taken hold of Kaelin's life and become a household word. Interminable waits in doctor's offices, hospital recovery rooms, medication schedule overloads, another night away from my family … you name it. I'm a problem-solver by nature and a sporadic complainer. As I look back on the last thirty-four years of Kaelin's life and almost—gulp—sixty-three years of *my* life, I realize that through it all the love of family and friends uplifted my spirit and helped me soar again.

My Gramma Lou and Gramma Fisher had what most folks would say were very hard lives. Widows at young ages with young children, no health insurance, the Depression era … but did they know how to live!

They lived frugally and with joy in abundance. These wonderful teachers set lasting examples that life is a daily event and we have no choice but to show up, and when you DO show up … put a smile on your face, a spring in your step, and a CAN-DO attitude—even on those days when you're worried sick or scared to death!

What does this have to do with lanyards and nametags? Kinda that full circle thing I'd say ... teachers and classrooms come in all shapes and sizes, whether a large conference hall filled with doctors, or around a kitchen table telling shaggy dog stories, or just playing cards.

THANK YOU for being another teacher in my life and for allowing me into yours in some small way. Each event, shared meal, or a knowing smile marks a moment in time that warms the heart and can find me saying it truly IS a Wonderful Life!

Love in the Time of Corona, COVID-19, or China ...

Well, this pandemic has been around long enough and generated fear with all the hype on many fronts. Don't get me wrong; caution IS a good thing and in moderation, otherwise the ad nauseam 24/7 newsfeed will create anxiety and much more. Let's put it in perspective!

Do you recall the moment your child was born with Sturge-Weber syndrome (SWS) or a Port Wine birthmark? I do. VIVIDLY! Our world started spinning out of control because back then we had no clue what caused the birthmark or SWS. I'm willing to bet many of you can recall too. In light of the severity of all that SWS can bring with its diagnosis, I hope you have been able to put this time of Corona in perspective and live life in gratitude. I know, it's weird to say gratitude, and I'm not exactly a Pollyanna—but I DO try my best to live in joy and gratitude every day.

Think about it ... SWS or Coronavirus or any other "crisis" can rob each of us if we let it! Sure, there are moments in a crisis that make us paralyzed with fear. I believe we need to take a deep breath and exhale through those moments. Get to the other side ... focus on love. I can't help but think about those of you getting your child ready for yet another glaucoma surgery, a brain surgery, or a trek to rehab as the media hype of fear ramps up. You know what a *real* crisis is and you know how to manage it!

I have a friend that has basically been quarantined off and on for over a year due to his cancer treatments before he went to heaven. Doug and Pat stayed optimistic and live life in love and faith. They and you remind me ... this too shall pass, and we only have THIS day to make a memory, and once the sun goes down we need to wake up and make more. You are best equipped to handle this time of Coronavirus because SWS has taught you how to be a warrior and keep on fighting.

Hang in there with all the school closings and social distancing, but please don't hoard! This too shall pass. We will remember the loving acts of kindness and support that will see us through, just as you and those around you have been doing with any SWS related surgery or crisis. The SWF and I will be here for you in good times and in bad, as always. Be well and love one another!

Just a few reminders of how to cope in crisis, Fisher style:

Freedom Isn't Free!

True. True. True. Fourth of July is always a special holiday for me and our family. We not only celebrate the brave men and women who KEEP us free with their sacrifices and courage, but our great country which has so many opportunities for those willing to sacrifice and stay the course. We also celebrate all those men, women, families, and professionals that create and uphold cherished freedoms for those living with a Sturge-Weber syndrome diagnosis. Yes, they forge freedoms for us every day!

I don't know if you've ever thought of this holiday in that way or not, but I was raised with a Daddy and uncles who served in the military service so I've always looked at SWS like my personal frontline. A war we HAVE to win and WILL win at all cost! We have had and still do have strategic plans that guide us into the battle against seizures, glaucoma, and birthmark treatments. The plans also include strategies for volunteer/staffing and funding. I am inspired by those who give it their all, whether on the frontlines of a war far from our shores or for a cause they deeply believe in and they never give up on.

Freedom from Worry. Learning about SWS and birthmarks, and about the SWS progression, and how to stay focused on the present in any given moment helps pinpoint what to worry about and what to let go. The SWF and our twenty-six Clinical Care Center staff can answer the questions that foment our worry (which leads to fear), so we can find moments to exhale in relief.

Freedom from Fear. Healthcare professionals and other families who share their hard-won wisdom as to how to overcome medical challenges or emotional ups and downs provide freedom from fear. Fear must be faced or the enemy wins.

Freedom to Hope. Researchers who are committed to doing basic and clinical research on SWS or birthmarks and finding innovative ways to think about the disease progression, psychological impacts, etc. give me—and I trust you, too—freedom to hope. Hope IS contagious!

Freedom to Believe. Families pulling together—whether in person or via social internet sites—sharing their lives, hopes, and dreams, provide us the freedom to believe that our world, which was rocked when we heard the first diagnosis, will find a new sense of normal. Believe with all your might!

Freedom is won and preserved by the vigilant and valiant warriors on the front lines and with the support teams who stand behind them. I know with a plan in hand, the right troops with you—be they doctors, relatives, friends, and more—you can and WILL win your battles and war.

Stay the Course. Celebrate with abandon, especially on holidays like July 4, as we ALL come together with patriotism, pride, and the knowledge that united we are stronger than divided!

Be Worthy!

It was a subdued Memorial Day weekend. For several years, I have been going to the Monarch Pass Memorial event with our dear friends Jim and Cathy. Jim received a Bronze Star in Vietnam, and through his sacrifices then and today—as he counsels suicidal vets—he is the persona of "Be Worthy." This phrase has really started to resonate with me as I reflect on our veterans and those people we've lost in the SWS fight. Veterans who have survived unspeakable times use this phrase to remember those gone and focus on living a life to honor them.

Am I worthy of the sacrifices they've made? Am I worthy and do I honor those on the early frontlines with SWS who have passed on, or do I just give lip service? Aaron Novak. Chad Layman. Danny Keffer. Noel Gelfund. Karen Sebastian. Christian Sarver. Michael Crouch. Nicole Meurin. Paul Siegel, Vida Garcia-Infante, Ava Duchene, Gordon Lunt, Shaun Byrne, Lonnie Herndon, Calvin Hubling, George MacDonald, Lakshmi Menon. So many more! So many SWS warriors who bravely fought against the ravaging seizures that took their lives too soon, and without the critical funding to find out why.

Am I worthy of supporting our own SWS and birthmark frontline doctors and researchers who give of their time and talents? They sacrifice time with their families to share time to enrich our loved ones' lives—and thereby ours. I am forever grateful!

Love. Honor. Sacrifice. Humble.

Thanks to generous donations and longtime dedicated supporters, the Sturge-Weber Foundation has led the way in finding the GNAQ gene mutation that causes SWS, engaging key researchers, developing clinical guidelines, and bringing families together for comfort and care. More can and should be done to honor the fallen and the living who still have far too many days in hospitals, struggle to walk, lose vision, and require special education.

Be Worthy.

They need you. I need you.

It's the commitment of time, talents, and treasure. Some days are better than others and there is no time. Some years are better than others and there is no money. It's the dedicated commitment to service and honor that's key. Together we have come a long way in thirty-four years ... together we will continue to assist those living with SWS and birthmarks every day, in every way.

Whipping or Whispering Winds ... the Storms of Life!

This view from my parents front deck has solved a lot of the world's problems, saw many a tear fall down our faces in joy and sorrow, and put up with some of the shaggiest of dog stories you've ever heard! I was sitting on the deck contemplating this awesome view when a big wind whipped up through the lodgepole pines. My mom commented that they can get some awful windstorms come through that make the pines REALLY whip around to and fro, and then my dad made an interesting comment. He said, "Kar, the winds do come in fast and furious and you see all the trees help disperse the wind and make the impact less on all of them." I can tell you that at ninety-one years of age he's seen a LOT of wind in his time, both literally and figuratively! That's why we lovingly refer to him as MOO (Mighty Omnipotent One).

Our SWF members and partners are the trees that help all of us disperse the fast and furious winds Sturge-Weber syndrome can send our way. Some of us face harsher storms in life depending on the reason or season. I know, like the winds whipping through those lodgepole pines, you make each windstorm easier to bear because you care and share all your wisdom with each other. Thank you for watching out for each other and encouraging one another either online, via email, or by phone. Together we are surviving deep worries and doing amazing things! Myla's Mission is the fiscal year kick-off fundraising event, and while virtual this year you all are doing an AWESOME job!

Exciting news! Because of all your financial and volunteer support, the SWF fostered and funded new researchers who have gone on to receive NIH grants to investigate SWS in zebrafish and mice, and to research two new compounds! The pace of discovery will exponentially increase once the zebrafish and mice develop ... compounds can be tested, and pathways and proteins too. While COVID-19 has put a storm in our path, we have all weathered it with grace and fortitude. The valuable support you give to one another and loved ones minimizes the hit from the whipping or whispering winds of change! Hang in there, and let's look forward to more exciting news and opportunities to be together again in person. Be safe and be well!

The photos above were taken in 2012 after Hurricane Sandy in New Jersey. Eight days, no power, and cold—but intrepid as always, the Ball family weathered those whipping winds too. Just remember: Even if your world and roots get upended, you ALWAYS have a choice to replant or make firewood ... all good and to handle it with grace and faith or lack thereof!

Seed Money and You: The Rippling Impact

Say it fast: thirty-three years! As we are entering our thirty-fourth year of offering comprehensive personalized services, support, and research funding, I want to share with you in a series of articles the rippling impact seed money and you have had around the world!

When I think back to the first "seed money"—you know, the kind of money where you gather a small amount to either fund your child's college fund, maybe save to buy your first home, or in the case of the SWF, save it up to bring families from around the country to the first International Conference or to fund research.

I hear many times from individuals "Well, I only have $25. I wish it could be more!" So, this lil' tome is my way of thanking you and impressing upon you how EVERY dollar donated counts and HAS had a VERY huge impact over the years. I marvel at those who hit the send button from Sudan, South Africa, Omaha, Nebraska, and thousands of other homes around the world ... all seeking support and direction for themselves or their loved one. Let me give you a few examples to illustrate my point:

Part 1: The Rippling Impact of Networking

Network and Support

I remember the very first mama who was like me (do you remember yours?). Before that conversation I thought I was the only one with a child with SWS and a birthmark on her face. I had NO idea how to help her or navigate the world in which I was then living in and would for a lifetime. I have been hesitant over the years when visiting with another mom or dad about SWS to say those words... a lifetime. Truth is though, the impact of a birthmark or an SWS diagnosis IS for a lifetime. Some of us dodge the proverbial bullet and the medical issues are slight if any, but the reality is we are inevitably changed due to the rippling impact the diagnosis has on our world and on those around us.

Seed money—sometimes scraped together by families hosting a special event or given in hope for a better world for their loved one or someone they know—has had a profound impact on the SWF's ability to bring you all together face to face, to share your journey, offer encouragement and hope, and share tidbits on coping, medication administration, and just life... you know, "My kid is driving me crazy" or "SOOOOO EXCITED she walked last week!" The SWF carefully saved and invested your seed money to host conferences and educational forums, sponsor events, and more so your world would become a little less scary, more informed, and more confident in handling anything SWS or a birthmark would throw your way.

"Friend" Raisers and Awareness

Along the way, Melanie Wood and Kathy Keffer led early fundraising events in their local communities, which kept donations flowing to replenish the coffers and to build a corpus of funds for the next patient conference and research seed grants. Families and individuals sent in donations and held garage sales and more to improve the quality of life and care for diagnosed individuals. Pamela McIntyre and Jessica Melo liked to run, so the Falmouth Road Race began!

Mark and Kelly Kenney and Meg O'Leary Hopkins loved football and Thanksgiving ... voila, The Turkey Bowl! Todd and Jackie Brown loved horse racing and golf, so together with Dr. David Brown and Dick Droesch we had our first racing horse and golf tournament!

These long-term events have had a HUGE impact on our ability to keep the SWF viable for the next family and next research investigator in need of funds. They have enabled those of us in medical or financial constraints to take time out so we too can honor those living with SWS, KT, or a birthmark, and host our own "give back and hand up" special events. Routes to a Cure Walks and Online Mobile Cause pages make it easier than ever! So many more of you volunteer at education conferences, on Capitol Hill, and thankfully there are not enough pages to list everyone, but I am personally grateful and humbled. Boards of Directors over the years donated countless hours to ensure the SWF maintained fiscal and governance accountability. Lauris Partizian and Valerie Lano volunteered for years when the SWF desperately needed administrative help but didn't have the funds for staff. Ian Hubling was our first webmaster. His technological ability made it possible for the world to become much smaller and for you to connect with others who spoke your language or had similar issues ... snail mail be GONE! They have earned gold-tipped wings in heaven!

Never underestimate what a committed few can do for you ... OR what more can be accomplished with MORE of you on the frontlines in our war on SWS! THANK YOU!

SWF parent Chris Spice and me at a Star Wars event for awareness.

YOU make it possible for their earnest pleas to be read, heard, and answered ... every day the SWF is juggling calls from families: "Who can I see about?" "Where can I get...?" "Is there a cure?" "I'm just so scared and frustrated, how do I cope?"—and more diverse questions.

YOU make it possible to maintain a world-class cadre of clinicians and scientists to fight on the frontlines of our war on SWS and birthmarks! They annually convene to set strategic research goals and funding needs, share ideas for collaborations and case studies, and get energized when they hear the latest reports on progress being made.

YOU make the SWF advocacy and awareness possible because you care and have committed yourself to our cause and uplift a world-class army of Champions that are living a more hopeful life and one focused on a brighter future. Thank YOU!

The world has gotten much smaller since 1987 and the days of "snail mail" and expensive long-distance telephone calls! Pick up your phone and Facetime your newfound SWF friend or shoot them an email or Facebook post for a quick answer to your query! If one isn't aware, the plethora of resources available and all those networks managed by the SWF could be taken for granted. Increased knowledge requires personal fortitude and one would hope a desire to share it with others. We have seen newly diagnosed patients take on amazing leadership roles within the SWF and I'm so proud of them!

The online and social media platforms provide unimaginable resources in need of careful vetting. The SWF takes a leadership role in being the vanguard on your behalf—a trusted resource of knowledge. There is a natural evolution of confidence that occurs after a diagnosis, especially with so many resources available. We've seen people come for assistance and families to network with when they are in their first crisis, and then they disappear for ten years, only to resurface when another aspect of SWS occurs or their now-teenage child is having emotional issues.

The SWF motto, "For a reason, a season, or a lifetime," was chosen to reflect the progressive nature of the syndrome as well as for our own emotional evolution in coping with the syndrome.

But make no mistake ... you do need the SWF for a lifetime. I am hesitant to say that to young parents lest it be perceived as hopeless and a life sentence.

The SWF is needed ... to keep advancing the science and clinical care for our loved ones and those who come after us.

The SWF is wanted ... to keep bringing families together to create bonds of friendship.

The SWF is required ... to advocate and generate awareness for those who need a wider voice.

The SWF is YOU!!! Stay involved.... The further we reach out, the closer we become.

The rippling impact of your cherished participation and vital seed money—minimal or vast—has made the SWF a beacon of hope for those who are confused and afraid, and improved our ability to reach across the world to walk in partnership with them—and together create more confident and compassionate families.

Part 2: The Rippling Impact of Collaboration and Research

It all started innocently enough, much as the roots of the Foundation did—a spark of knowing what needed to happen! So, after about a year of answering people's mail and phone calls I figured, "Well, let's try and get these people together." I wrote an article for *The Denver Post* on Sturge-Weber syndrome, Kaelin, and the fledgling Sturge-Weber Foundation.

While Kaelin was napping, I was sitting at my Amoco-donated desk (that I still use today) in my unfinished basement in the oh-so-elegant office attire of sweatpants and t-shirt when a telephone call came in: "Hello, this is Betty Ford's secretary, and she'd like to honor you...." Uh, yeah ... right ... click! A minute later it rang again. "Please don't hang up!" And the rest is history:

The Sturge-Weber Foundation Research Fund was established with the First Lady Betty Ford Award donation for tenacity in the face of adversity and this small "seed grant" of $5,000 which was to be the corpus of research funding.

$5,000: First Lady Betty Ford Award

The Former First Lady Betty Ford was being honored by the Beaver Creek Hyatt and she wanted to share the event with those who had tenacity in the face of adversity. Jim and Sarah Brady were the national honorees and Kirk and I were the Colorado honorees. HUGE gala and cocktails at the Ford's home and many new contacts made to help along the way. The most important moment though was when we were surprised with the $5,000 award check. Our annual budget was $2,500! The further we reach out ... the closer we become! Just go for it—you'll never know, and we need an ARMY of Champions like you and President and Mrs. Ford to maintain the momentum until there are no more children born with SWS!

Volunteers and $30,000 Seed Research Grant

The years flew by while Kaelin stabilized her glaucoma and seizures and the Foundation had an Access database registry of 400 cases of diagnosed SWS. The office moved from my home to a small office with a part-time administrative assistant, Marsha Dingbaum (who still donates today!) to help juggle the workload. Two young mothers, working around naptime and school schedules, to connect with other people impacted by a diagnosis and in need of support.

Volunteers

Doctors Bill Weston, Joe Morelli, and Allan Eisenbaum provided expert medical advice and propagated awareness on TV and in print. Dr. Eva Sujansky and colleagues published medical journal articles based on the information I had recorded during support telephone calls from the 400 families. Back then, patient advocates were not being recognized as authors on papers or I would have another two papers to my credit! Dr. Richard Finkel put flyers on SWS and the SWF in the bags of doctors attending the Child Neurology Society annual meeting, inviting them to a meeting to discuss plans for clinical studies. Doctors Steve Roach, John Bodensteiner, and Harry Chugani took the reins and we were off! They amassed a Medical Advisory Board to write articles, give lectures, review research grant proposals, and extend the "SWS experts" around the country. Today we have thousands of healthcare providers in our database and young clinicians being trained around the country and abroad to care for our patients. Of course, as if that wasn't

Dr. Harry T. Chugani, MD, and the author.

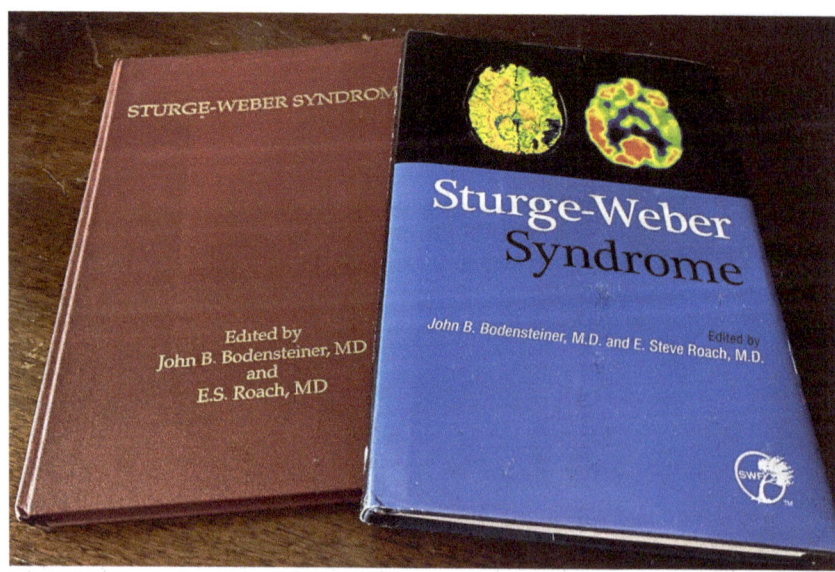

The First Edition of Sturge-Weber syndrome was published in June 1999.

enough, they decided we needed to publish the first SWS textbook in forty years and with Alberta Edwards' able guidance we did. The second edition is still available to order online.

$30,000: Seed Grant

Doctor Bernie Maria received the first research grant: seed money to make an impact on our understanding of SWS. All your generous donations were carefully saved and spent, which enabled us to bring more hands on deck to foster more awareness, discuss clinical studies, and attend medical conferences to engage more clinical and research care providers and investigators. The seed grant also let the medical community know that the SWF and our supporters were serious about making strides in our understanding and ultimate goal to find the cause.

$50,000: A Center of Excellence to Clinical Care Network—Rippling Impact

The next phase of organizational growth brought a move to New Jersey and the addition of more staff to handle communication, patient and caregiver networks, and "friend"-raising special events. It became apparent the SWF needed to expand the knowledge base and establish targeted endeavors to shape research. The SWF awarded a $50,000 seed grant to establish a Center of Excellence (COE) at Johns Hopkins Hospital, with Dr. Anne Comi directing that initial center. The first SWF COE proved to be a good working model and we appreciate Dr. Comi for her dedication; we've continued to work with her long after she chose to become an independent and self-funded center. As the SWF membership grew and evolved, we recognized the need to minimize daily life disruptions and the financial burden for families having to travel across country in some cases. We began to expand the renamed Clinical Care Network facilities across the country at key universities and hospitals that were committed to excellence in care and research. Today there are over twenty-six CCN facilities and a burgeoning cadre of young professionals.

Good Guys! Dr. Jonathan Pevsner and Grant Fisher.

$25,000: Data Needs a Registry

With the growth of new software programs, those first eleven-by-seventeen papers where I recorded vital statistical data collected from patient-reported information were entered into an Access database. We maintained this data in Access for many years and expanded what we recorded based on the influx of reports by patients. Little did we know we had a "registry." Today registries are numerous, online, and cover a variety of data collected. The registry requires $25,000 annually to maintain, data mine, and engage patient participation. My dad used to say, "From little acorns grow mighty oaks"—no truer words have been spoken! Your vigilance in sharing the natural history of SWS in your life along, with thousands of others who have been diagnosed, has shaped our understanding of the course of the disease and treatment.

The corpus of data collected over the years has been used as documentation in many medical journal articles, helping to educate a new generation of caregivers and researchers. The profound impact of gathering data and sharing the statistical data, all while engaging clinicians and researchers, has opened up new fields of study and enlightened families and caregivers alike. THANK YOU!

$40,000: NIH CSO and Multi-million Dollar BVMC

The rippling impact of being responsible stewards of the compounding donations gave us the ability to fund the SWF's first Chief Scientific Officer (CSO), who was a former program officer at the National Institutes of Health (NIH). This investment provided strategic leadership and established the first strategic research plan to guide us in setting goals and action items. Our CSO's knowledge of the NIH grants and review committees positioned us to submit for what was in 2008 an emerging mechanism of funding to establish Consortiums. These consortiums consisted of three disease groups that shared a similar issue. In our case, it was and is brain vascular malformations (BVMC).

Without your hard-earned and generous donations, the SWF would not have been in a financial position to hire an expert to coalesce and collaborate with an amazing team of scientists. Thanks to the NIH, our Sturge-Weber staff and team of researchers, and patients participating in research and tissue donation, the cause of SWS with the GNAQ gene discovery was made in 2013. A dream come true ... for a reason, a season, or a lifetime!

Dr. Bodensteiner and Dr. Loeb with the author.

$50,000: And Another Young Investigator Off and Running

Dr. E. Steve Roach.

Lisa's Research Fellowship was established in 2015 to support young investigators and to build a new generation of Sturge-Weber syndrome key opinion leaders. The humble and faithful family who established the fund gave all of us an immense gift that will have impact long after we are gone. Investing in the future of clinical care and scientific investigations is key to maintaining the momentum since our incorporation. Each of us doing our part, whether minimal or vast, increases the pace of discovery and brings us closer together! Why $50,000? A fellowship pays their salary so they can work with a mentor and investigate their hypothesis, which oftentimes leads to new discoveries and treatments. It's an investment in our future and theirs!

The Sturge-Weber Foundation International Research Network (SWFIRN) and Patient Engagement Network (PEN)

The SWFIRN and PEN met in September 2016 to discuss research needs and best practices and to establish strategic research goals. Participants came from around the world to unite and ignite collaborations to drive discovery. This meeting was possible because the National Institutes of Health (NIH) invested in patient participation through the Patient Centered Outcomes Research Initiative (PCORI), which promotes patient input as integral to propagating ethical and effective research. Brian J. Fisher, SWF's vice-president of Operations and Corporate Partnerships, secured the PCORI grant, which also brought industry leaders who participated with exciting collaborations between attendees and the SWF currently in development! Regularly scheduled teleconferences keep everyone on task and united, so your hope for answers or direction becomes a reality created through improved quality of care and treatments. Yesterday, Today, and for the Future—the rippling impact of your time, talent, and donations proportionately impacts the world around us! Stay in touch! Stay involved! You will ALWAYS be needed and matter!

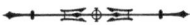

Part 3: The Rippling Impact of Investing in Infrastructure

The rippling impact of your participation in research, the registry, and financial support has enabled the SWF to seek out from around the world the best and brightest clinicians and scientists to jump-start a career, to launch a SWFIRN for global collaboration, and to fund promising investigations to find the cause of SWS and more!

Unfinished Basement

So, the truth is the SWF actually started in a spare bedroom in our first home. Kaelin took her naps and I answered "snail mail" or made phone calls to physicians requesting their help. Thanks to donated Amoco office furniture of a desk, file cabinet, office chair, and electric typewriter, I was able to move the office to our downstairs unfinished basement when files and supplies outgrew the bedroom space. I was so caught up in ensuring we had enough money from the donations trickling in to deliver support via the mail and a phone line, and to develop a healthcare provider resource list, that it never crossed my mind or Kirk's to reimburse ourselves for the use of electricity or increased long-distance phone bill (yes, we actually had to pay for long distance charges in the dark ages!).

Families were in need, and while donations were slowly coming in after incorporation in September 1987, there weren't enough donations to cover mailings, newsletter printing, etc. AND pay the utilities—let alone to pay for my time. There were increasing days when I had to meet doctors or give interviews when Kaelin wasn't napping. With a HUGE plethora of medical bills and doctor visits to pay for we couldn't afford to pay for babysitters AND utilities too. I finally relented and took a "salary" equal only to the babysitting costs and burgeoning telephone bills that were required to conduct the SWF business.

More and more people were learning of the SWF via their doctors, and slowly the case files grew (yes, only paper back then)—and donations did too! The Board of Directors approved the hire of a part-time administrative assistant and office space. H-U-G-E leap of faith for the organization and me personally, as I had to leave Kaelin a few days a week with her preschool teacher, Sue Furia, so I could keep up with inquiries and demands. I always wanted to be a stay-at-home mom, but clearly God had other plans!

Part-Time Administrative Assistant/Office Space/Volunteers

Infrastructure isn't a "sexy" program to think about or to fund, but it is absolutely essential to meet demand for services, awareness, networking, and research. Without hands on deck and funding to keep them there, the ability to support those in need and the pace of discovery will grind to a glacial pace or even halt. The Board's approval to hire the administrative assistant and to get the office was key to the SWF's ability to keep the momentum going and position the organization to eventually fund research. We had more than 400 identified cases of Sturge-Weber when we relocated to official office space. Lots of file cabinets and thankfully another typewriter to keep pace with press inquiries and brochure mailings to families and healthcare providers.

We also had the ability to plan our first family conference and all the logistics that entailed. Basically, we were really off and running!

SWS advocates on Capitol Hill.

The Betty Ford Award helped us reach a wider audience and the Ann Landers column answering Anita Messer's letter doubled our membership overnight. I remember the call from Ms. Lander's assistant, asking us if we had the ability to answer the letters we would receive. Of course, I eagerly and naively told her yes! Thank goodness for the wisdom of my elders and family! My aunt and uncle, Carlene and Bruce Fisher, came over and triaged the 400-plus letters and new families to welcome, making our member total 800! We placed the letters into regional piles so we could respond with regionally based information. With their help, our volunteers now numbered six, along with our Board members Don Hanley, Stan Fisher, Pete Ober, and Kirk Ball! My Daddy always says, "Many hands make light work."

Truist Park, home of the Atlanta Braves photo, who hosted the Sturge-Weber Foundation's Family Game Day on May 22, 2021 for nearly 30 families.

Part 4: The Future Harvest

Today not-for-profit startups have a plethora of online platforms, software, and software integration that make it more efficient and streamlined to communicate. The ease with which an organization can reach out to other not-for-profits (NPOs) for advice is amazing! Back in the dark ages when NPOs were really just emerging, especially in the rare disease space, there were not as many resources to access. We relied on the spirit of generosity to share our collective knowledge of governance, education, patient support, etc. Online social media forums have "been there, done that" expert parental advice that still needs to be tempered with reminders each case of SWS, KT, and birthmark issues are unique, and while experiences shared are a great comfort, they are not your personal journey or your medical matter.

The Further We Reach Out, the Closer We Become

SWF has benefited every day from all the latest technology and social media venues as we tailor-fit our responses to your inquiries.

New volunteers continue to step up to give back to all of us! Chris and Dana Davis supported the new website, which is an internationally respected and vetted resource for patients and caregivers alike. The adjustment from traditional office to a blend of traditional and remote workers who interface with volunteers around the world has put the SWF in a perfect position for rapid response. The tailor-fit service, online forums, and vast network of resources ensures you ARE in good hands!

As donations and grants are received, the SWF is able to expand services and programs with knowledgeable staff and volunteers working together to foster the vision and mission. I know what I know, and I know what I don't know! I have never been afraid to admit I don't know ... which is why I search out the world to find the brightest researchers and clinicians, volunteers, and staff to forge new inroads and plant new seeds of thought and hope.

Healthcare Providers and Investigators

Yesterday's scientists and clinicians are training a new frontline of investigators. They are utilizing technology and our vastly increased understanding of SWS, KT, and birthmarks since the dark ages of 1986 to improve the quality of care and increase the pace of discovery. Lisa's Research Fellowship, provided by Lisa P. and her parents, Steve and Melanie, has fostered excitement for young investigators and increased collaborations. Fellowship recipients then apply to the National Institutes of Health (NIH) for larger grant awards.

With over twenty-six SWF Clinical Care Network (CCN) facilities throughout the U.S., individuals and parents no longer have to trek across country from one coast to the other like I did with Kaelin in 1987. They can rest assured that these CCN facilities have dedicated and knowledgeable staff who will provide the best care and collaborate with researchers around the world. The blend of national facilities with various areas of expertise ensures that collaborations among the CCN and with those from beyond the CCN will keep the SWS clinical and scientific research burgeoning for years to come.

I realize how blessed I've been and how fortunate the SWF has been to have so many dedicated volunteers and families as I look back over thirty-four years of service and support. I live in hope that new families with a diagnosed loved one and individuals living with a diagnosis don't take for granted all that has been planted so far. While we continually harvest the fruits of our labors, we need individuals to step up and nurture the SWF with their time, talents, and treasure. Your attention and commitment will ensure that the next generation (until we eradicate SWS, KT, and birthmarks) will have just as robust if not more resources and committed collaborators! Together we have created amazing opportunities and accomplished hoped-for and even unimagined goals. Please do even just one thing with who and what you know.... Champions are made, not born!

Yesterday, Today, and for the Future ... the rippling impact of your time, talent, and donations proportionately impacts the world around us!

On the Road of Life and Love

I had just come back from an amazing SWF Educational Forum in Detroit and was glancing out my window as I reflected on the wonderful attendees and speakers. How lucky I am to be privileged to share in their lives and share stories of love with them. My contact at the hotel was Robert—very nice and detail oriented. Miles, the A/V man, treated us the same as if we were a Fortune 500 company. I realized as I gazed out the window that we have front row seats to events that change people's lives.

Out the window, I could see Robert was overseeing the garden wedding of a young couple just starting their life together. The life events and years ahead are unknown yet easier to bear with your best friend, spouse, and family with you. With a SWS diagnosis, family, friends, and healthcare providers see us through it one day at a time. The Forum, like the wedding I was observing, brought together people wanting to share a moment in time to connect, care, and inspire each other. At the Forum, we had two families who met at the doctor's office and used to work together, now forever linked by children with SWS. Young, old, and in-between—each unique, yet still so clearly seen with loving eyes and hearts.

Everywhere I go around the world—whether in San Francisco reconnecting with longtime SWF members and friends, or in Ireland bringing new SWF friends together—I am so lucky! Thank you for sharing your stories with me... they keep me inspired and motivated. Thank you for shedding your tears and fears... they keep us mindful to live in joy. Thank you for caring not only about your loved one but those currently diagnosed and those lil' ones on the way... you keep us connected and cherished.

Every time we are together and reach out to one another we bring light and hope into the world and keep the darkness at bay. Whether you are like the young, married couple just starting out or you have been down the road with SWS for years, *the further we reach out the closer we become!* These cherished baby shoes that were my Mama's and my Great Gramma's glasses remind me that our stories begin at home. We will always have big shoes to fill and can see the world with more discerning and hopeful eyes when we have the love and support of family. May God bless you and yours as he has our family!

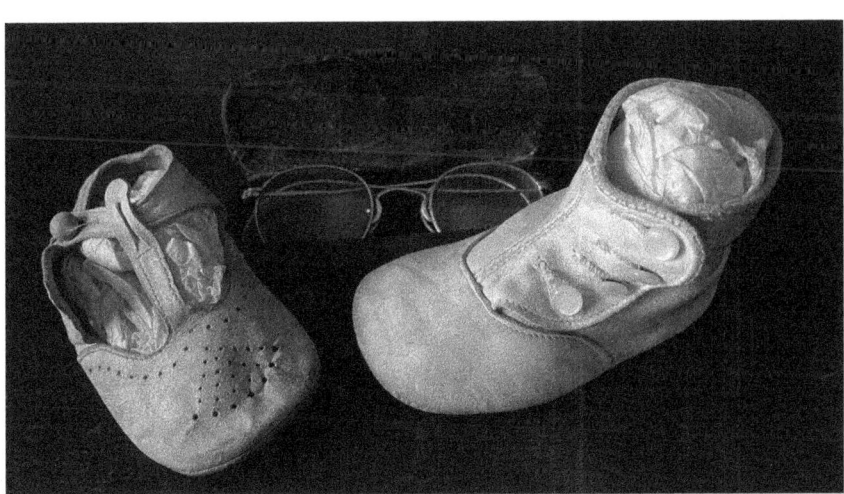

Kaelin greets her brother Derek.

Your Personal Day of Infamy or Epiphany

My personal day of infamy came on October 11, 1986. It was the day my daughter, Kaelin, was born and became a patient being treated for Sturge-Weber syndrome with glaucoma and a Port Wine birthmark as the outward signs of potential cranial involvement and all that it implies. A mother's first pregnancy is filled with wonder and anticipation, with a smidgeon of nerves for the unknown. The attending physician wisely decided that, after two weeks post-due date, a C-section was in order and Kaelin weighed in at nine pounds, fourteen and three-quarter ounces!

The world of myriad unknowns with a SWS diagnosis came crashing in on all of us as she was rushed from my arms for glaucoma treatment by a thankfully amazing local glaucoma specialist. This was followed by a release from the hospital a week later to go directly to his office for a pre-op visit, and THEN we could take our first-born home to "celebrate" her arrival. Our lives have never been normal ever since, but I believe the ability to face adversity and find humor amidst the chaos, financial strains, and shifting treatment options has made us stronger people. I know it has for my daughter.

Three glaucoma surgeries in the first three months of life. Seizures at a year. Glaucoma in her other eye at five years old and numerous surgeries for that eye and a severe bout of depression in her early twenties due to being bedridden for three months post-glaucoma surgery low-pressure issues. She has weathered it all with grace and a compassionate heart for those living with SWS who are much more severely affected by the neurological and cognitive challenges of daily living with SWS. Today she has a Master's Degree and lives a fairly independent life and has dedicated herself to educating all those who will hear her story.

Her standard for facing adversity was set early on when we went to a fundraiser in Pittsburgh for Danny Keffer. Danny had bilateral SWS and valiantly fought his way through life not speaking but having his wants and need being LOUDLY heard. He never walked or talked, had brittle bones and numerous infusions before he passed

College Graduation #1.

away at thirty. Thirty years of lifting him up, feeding him, ER visits, medications, and diaper changes ... his mom was and is a saint. Kaelin always said if Danny and his mom Kathy can do it, I can too. It is this standard bearer of grace amidst adversity we have always strived to imbibe in Kaelin and all those we serve at the Sturge-Weber Foundation. Yes you can—one second, one minute, one hour, one day at a time ... but you CAN endure and thrive!

We all have a day of infamy if we really think about it. It might be a personal medical issue, a divorce in the family, a financial strain, or sadly early death of a child or parent, but we ALL face adversity. What brings us here to offer our wisdom and compassion is uniquely our story to tell and that adversity shaped who YOU are today. Together we have pledged to improve the quality of life and care for those living with severely debilitating vascular malformations and volunteer what we have been blessed to know and learn from our betters to ensure we fund the best and brightest. Thank you for being committed to your family, patients, research, loved ones, and those patients to come. Join me in a moment of silence as we honor and uplift them all. Thank you.

The Only Recipe to Remember!

I find great comfort in baking and cooking for people. I pull out the ingredients from the cupboard and fridge, and from memory I measure the right amount of each part of the recipe into the bowl. I'll bet y'all have some traditional and favorite recipes you use every holiday or birthday celebration too. What's fun is to mix and match the family handed-down, generation-to-generation recipes with those new recipes shared by friends along the way.

The Foundation comforts me in the same way as those recipes! I have dear friends from thirty-two years with whom I've shared recipes and family experiences. When I remember cherished days spent

fundraising, educating the public, and more often than not sharing a laugh to break the tension of sadness or to bring each other to tears of joy—that's a fabulous recipe for comfort! There are also friends met along the way in the medical profession, educators, parents, industry, government, and so many more who with their own special compassion, dedication, and life experiences have enriched my life's table too ... a terrific recipe for inspiration!

We recently lost a great chef! The NIAMS Director, Dr. Steve Katz at the National Institutes of Health, could whip up some terrific recipes of collaboration! He enriched our lives with his foresight to bring special people and ingredients together, which made amazing strides for research! He did it with the only recipe we need to remember, too! He will be truly missed and we have been forever changed by his presence.

The only recipe to really remember is the shortest and simplest to make. It starts and ends with only one ingredient that matters ... it keeps on giving! What makes the greatest impact for any recipe or encounter is, of course, to add in ... Love. If we start with that simple, one-ingredient recipe, the sweetest moments will rise up and fill the holes and hurts. Love generates hope in hopeless situations. Love uplifts and gives us energy to carry on.

When I was a lil' chubby kid, my Aunt Joan gave me that recipe. She saw me and my chatty, bubbly, joy-filled exuberance for life and reinforced that it's not what's on the outside that matters or will make for great feasts and moments, but loving myself for who I am and what I can give—it's the best recipe ever!

I wish you all a New Year filled with recipes that bring comfort, inspiration, and hope. I hope you have or will find those people like Dr. Katz and Aunt Joan that share their recipes with you too! I wish you good health and peace knowing the Foundation is here with the only recipe you need to remember ... Love!

Afterword

What a wonderful life it HAS been! The Sturge-Weber Foundation has grown up to become a respected and successful organization. Kaelin has become a beautiful young woman, ready to face her future of hopes and dreams to be robustly lived. I've learned to forgive myself for the missteps and hurts inflicted along the way and hope the good outweighs the bad. I'm also ready to begin structuring a life after SWF and to enjoy the path filled with mountain views too!

Those of us who have ever lived and walked this SWS Journey or known someone who has must continue to support both the SWF and those living with SWS every day. A new generation of diagnosed SWS patients and their families deserve the same tenacity, compassion, and curiosity that fueled us in the beginning. They deserve to live in hope, empowered through support and continued research, until there is a cure. They deserve to know they are valued and make our lives richer for their presence in it. Thank you for joining me on this remarkable journey and taking

The years tell us much that the days never knew!

the time to read the Tales from the Trails in this book. Together, we will continue to leave a lasting legacy for them!

Anyone who knows me well knows I LOVE photos. It was agony having to choose which photos to include and exclude, so the editor and I compromised. We wanted to keep a balance and flow for the reader and honor the lives well-lived with these cherished additional photos too.

Some photos are from our family and some are from the SWF family. I hope you enjoy them!

Afterword

One day, the mountain that is in front of you will be so far behind you, it will barely be visible in the distance.

But the person you become in learning to get over it will stay with you forever — and that is the point of the mountain.

— *Brianna Wiest*

About the Sturge-Weber Foundation

The Sturge-Weber Foundation (SWF) is a 501(c)3 non-profit organization that assists patients and families living with Sturge-Weber syndrome. The Foundation offers educational resources and events (virtual and in-person) to educate and inform all interested parties about progress in research and better treatments that improve quality of life. SWF's Clinical Care Network lists centers and physicians who specialize in treating SWS. The SWF International Research Network is a platform for researchers to collaborate and gain insight from other researchers studying the cause of SWS and seeking a potential cure.

The Foundation's website, www.sturge-weber.org, includes a library of resource material in both print and video formats. These resources are designed to help both the newly diagnosed as well as those transitioning from pediatric to adult care. Other website features include a peer-to-peer fundraising platform, volunteer opportunities, an events calendar, archives of recent quarterly newsletters, blogs from Karen Ball, and more.

We invite you to visit the website and learn more about SWS, what SWF does—and how you can be a part of it!

www.ingramcontent.com/pod-product-compliance
Lightning Source LLC
Chambersburg PA
CBHW062058290426
44110CB00022B/2629